A BACKGROUI

The Sino-Soviet Conflict

ELEVEN RADIO DISCUSSIONS

EDITED BY

Leopold Labedz
&
G. R. Urban

THE BODLEY HEAD

LONDON

© Radio Free Europe 1964, 1965
Printed and bound in Great Britain for
The Bodley Head Ltd
10 Earlham Street, London, WC2
by William Clowes & Sons Ltd, Beccles
Set in Linotype Plantin
First published 1965

Contents

NOTE

The Sino-Soviet Conflict was originally commissioned by Radio Free Europe as a series of round-table discussions. Ten of the eleven programmes were recorded in London in early 1964 and subsequently broadcast in Polish, Hungarian, Czech, Slovak, Rumanian and Bulgarian from the Munich studios of Radio Free Europe. The eleventh discussion, recorded and broadcast in December 1964, evaluates Khrushchev's dismissal and its probable consequences for the conflict between Moscow and Peking. Leopold Labedz's Introduction and Postscript bring the story up to June 1965. Editorial changes have been confined to removing repetitions, rephrasing some of the more colloquial passages in the original, and adding a few footnotes to cover some of the more recent events relevant to the points raised in the discussion whenever they seemed necessary to indicate the subsequent evolution of the conflict. However, references to people who have died or lost power in the meantime have not been updated.

6

Introduction

Leopold Labedz

It seems reasonably certain that future historians will look at the Sino-Soviet conflict as the most important development after the advent of the Cold War. But at present its far-reaching implications are only dimly perceived, and its observable consequences in international politics have not yet been analysed in a comprehensive study which would put the matter into historical perspective.

This volume is, of course, no such study. It is in any case too early for that. It runs the additional risk of all radio commentaries on the quickly changing international scene of being overtaken by events. Nevertheless, if that risk is being taken in publishing these discussions, it is because they were conceived and conducted not merely as topical commentaries on the current manifestations of the Sino-Soviet rivalry, but as occasions for analytical reflections on their more permanent significance. The discussions were focused on the wider aspects of the conflict, its impact on the international communist movement, and on international relations in general.

These discussions took place at the beginning of 1964 except for one that was added after Khrushchev's fall. It is up to the reader to judge how they have withstood the test of time, how subsequent developments have confirmed or refuted some of the assumptions made and some of the conclusions drawn by the participants.

The major event which is outside the body of the discussions is the outcome of the attempts by Khrushchev's successors to take the heat out of the Sino-Soviet dispute, to achieve at least a ban on public polemics between the two sides. This attempt failed. The Chinese leaders made it clear that they were not interested in any compromise, tacit or otherwise, and as ideological assaults were their most important weapon, they flatly rejected the idea of giving them up.

There was (and there is) no agreement among the observers about the depth of the Sino-Soviet split. After Khrushchev's fall many of them expected to see a reconciliation. The 'conciliators' among the 'ecumenical' communist leaders hoped all along that the quarrel would somehow be patched up. In June 1964, shortly after the radio discussions reproduced here were recorded, I happened to discuss the

7

subject (on an Australian television programme) with the secretary of the British Communist Party, John Gollan, who argued that there was no Sino-Soviet 'split', but only 'serious differences of opinion' between the two parties. These differences, Mr. Gollan confidently predicted, would soon be overcome.

That was at the time when the Sino-Soviet polemics were at their peak; Khrushchev was preparing to excommunicate the Chinese at a conference of the communist parties, and his fall was not yet in sight. There were yet to follow: the Togliatti memorandum, which dealt a death blow to the Soviet hopes of achieving an agreement among their supporters on the tactical measures to be taken against the Chinese; the postponement of the preparatory conference by Khrushchev's successors from its original date of December 15, 1964, to March 1, 1965; the degradation of the preparatory conference to a mere 'consultative' meeting; its melancholy outcome in the form of an empty communiqué; and finally the new Chinese blast against the Soviet 'Khrushchevite revisionists without Khrushchev' who dared to convene the conference even in this politically emasculated form.

While the Moscow conference of the 19 parties was in session, Chinese and other Asian students staged an attack against the American embassy in Moscow. The ensuing scuffles with the Soviet militiamen were certain to create maximum embarrassment to the Soviet sponsors of the conference, to 'expose' their inadequate commitment in Vietnam and their reluctance to get involved in a direct military confrontation with the United States in South-East Asia. China's tactics were clear and simple—a case of 'heads I win, tails you lose'. If the Russians let themselves be manœuvred into some sort of a frontal clash with America, it would be a case of China playing the *tertius gaudens* in the Soviet-American struggle. If, on the other hand, they refused to be pushed into it, they would be denounced for the betrayal of the revolutionary cause. As the previous Sino-Soviet polemics demonstrated, the Russians were perfectly well aware of the motives behind the Chinese manœuvres; they have been quite explicit about it. Their policy on Vietnam clearly reflected their efforts to avoid the dilemma. It was promptly denounced by the Chinese as anti-imperialist in words but anti-revolutionary in deeds.

The Chinese were also in a dilemma. They castigated the Russians for insufficient military aid to Ho Chi Minh, but they could not cherish the prospect of the increased Soviet military presence in South-East Asia which they regarded as their own sphere of interest. They were more militant, but militarily they had to be even more cautious. Their direct involvement in the Vietnamese war would leave Russia, and not themselves, in the position of *tertius gaudens*. Also their newly-built nuclear industry was highly vulnerable from the air.

In general, like Cuba and Ladakh previously, Vietnam demonstrated that for the split communist powers another military emergency did not lead to a 'greater solidarity against the imperialists'. It failed to produce a co-ordination of Sino-Soviet action; it only resulted in a more complicated political game accompanied by mutual recriminations. In a wider perspective it could only be regarded as another incident in the Sino-Soviet conflict, dividing the two countries still further, rather than cementing them.

The Sino-Soviet conflict is historically significant in many other respects: it marks the end of the unity, political and organizational, of the international communist movement; it ends the myth of 'proletarian internationalism' by showing that relations between the communist states may be no better, indeed they may be worse, than the relations between the states which profess no such elevated aims; it weakens the myth of 'historical inevitability', which gives 'true believers' the certainty of ultimate victory, and which has now become a subject of manifold and contradictory interpretations by different ideological centres. Its effects on the two main contestants themselves can only be divined, but they cannot fail to be far-reaching, deep and lasting.

It has often been said that 'foreign policy begins at home'. The statement can be misleading, particularly when it is applied to states based on revolutionary and not traditional legitimation. But the exclusive emphasis on external factors in the analysis of international relations may be no less of a half-truth. Clearly there is a reciprocal relationship between domestic and external factors which influences both home and foreign policy. This is true of all states, although in any given case one set of factors may be more important than the other.

If the Sino-Soviet conflict were merely the traditional rivalry between the two great powers, their ideological dispute and struggle for the loyalty of communists all over the world would be pretty well incomprehensible. And indeed, those students of history who in all cases see in the conduct of foreign policy nothing but an expression of a rationally conceived national interest tend to dismiss the ideological clash as only a smokescreen. In doing this they may be overlooking the problem of internal legitimation, necessary for the maintenance of the rule of the Communist Party at home, and of the external legitimation, necessary for the state which wants to have the additional strength it can derive (or thinks it can derive) from its support by foreign communist parties. And they may also be overlooking the element of *furor theologicus*, which, though not a rational factor, was real enough, for instance, in the European religious wars.

If, on the other hand, the Sino-Soviet conflict were nothing but a struggle for hegemony in the international communist movement, the two powers would simply be engaged in a test of militancy, and this is not the case. Their position and moves are obviously being shaped by a variety of factors.

From the beginning, the Soviet Communist Party faced the twin problems of orthodoxy and universality. Lenin's seizure of power in an economically backward country was not orthodox Marxism. Very soon the Bolsheviks were also confronted with sharp choices between the interests of their state and those of the revolutionary movements abroad. The new Leninist theory of revolution replaced the original Marxist one: it was no longer a question of waiting for the industrial society of the capitalist countries to generate the discontent which would bring about a socialist revolution, for now it was argued that a communist party could seize power in a backward country and create the conditions for a socialist society without waiting for capitalism to prepare its own downfall and pave the way for socialism. The universalistic aspirations were safeguarded by identifying the interests of the 'international revolution' with the interests of the Soviet state, invariably sacrificing the former, a process which culminated in Stalin's theory of 'socialism in one country' and his successful maintenance of the principle that the first duty of all communists was the defence of Soviet interests. Thus both historically and doctrinally communism and the Soviet Union were inseparable.

However, after the Second World War this was no longer the case, and the Soviet guardians of the doctrine found it more and more difficult to maintain its orthodoxy and universality. They were now facing not merely the clashes of interest between their state and those of revolutionary movements abroad, but clashes of interest between their own and those of other established communist states. It was no longer possible to pass off their own interests as universal, although they were trying, and the size of the problem grew from the defection of Yugoslavia to the Sino-Soviet conflict, bringing in its wake the intensification of the process of communist polycentrism and undermining completely the universal character of Soviet Marxism-Leninism.

At the same time there was a slow erosion of orthodoxy inside the Soviet Union. Leninism inherited from Marxism a utopian legacy which was increasingly contradicted by the facts of Soviet industrial development. It was becoming more and more clear that, whether society had nominally lost its class character or not, important differences in prestige, income, education and power also persisted in the Soviet type of society and that these were significant for social stratification. The 'withering away of the state', the end of 'alienation', the disappearance of the differences between manual and intellectual labour, and between urban and rural environments—all these were utopian propositions. The Marxist theory of value had become an obstacle in Soviet economics and is preventing a more modern approach to planning. The list can be continued, but the point here is not merely that chiliastic dreams were not, and were not likely to be, implemented after the communist seizure of power, but that it is increasingly difficult for the Soviet ideologists to maintain these fictions. It is not only that they have become an empty ritual abandoned in practice, but some of them at least are now challenged from within the orthodoxy, even in theory. For instance, some communist philosophers now openly admit that alienation will continue to exist in socialist society, the younger Soviet economists are tacitly, or even explicitly, rejecting the Marxist theory of value, and so on. In short, orthodoxy is being eroded and this is not unimportant for the future of party rule and the character of the state in which it is ruling.

It is against this background that one has to look at the 'theological' clash between the Maoist orthodoxy and what the Chinese refer to as Soviet 'revisionism'. The external dynamics of a state based on revolutionary legitimation, such as the Soviet Union, depend not only on the opportunities abroad, but also on the internal evolution which may sap its revolutionary momentum. This is of course a process which may still take a long time to mature, so that one must not draw any immediate political conclusions from it, but it is clearly relevant for the future, and it will both affect and be affected by the Sino-Soviet conflict and the communist polycentric developments in general.

In its main course the internal evolution of the Soviet and Chinese societies will of course continue independently of the Sino-Soviet conflict, but it can already be seen that some domestic developments in the two countries are influenced by it. For instance, Soviet writers enjoyed a welcome relief from the pressure of the party watchdogs on literature when they could use against them 'anti-dogmatic' arguments taken from the official polemics against the Chinese 'dogmatists'; conversely the Soviet 'conservatives' were anxious to dissociate themselves from such unwanted allies. Praise in the Chinese press is for them no less a 'kiss of death' than praise in the 'bourgeois' press is for the 'liberal' writers. The scholastic dispute on 'the historical character of our epoch'—in which the Chinese insist on the priority of the revolutionary struggle with 'imperialism' and the Russians on the priority of economic competition with 'capitalism'—has an obvious bearing not only on the question whether the Soviet Union should become an arsenal for revolutionary China or build its own economy faster, but also on the whole character of its evolution. A bending of Marxist doctrine is necessary if the Soviet economy is to move away from the Stalinist model of top-heavy industrial development, and economic revisionism in the Soviet Union can only benefit from the general 'anti-dogmatic' orientation which a dispute with China may help to stimulate.

In China, where the evolution of the post-revolutionary society has not gone very far and the economy is primitive, the effects of the conflict with Russia are more difficult to gauge. But it is pretty clear, for instance, that such momentous decisions as the 'great leap forward' and the introduction of communes were not unconnected with the Sino-Soviet conflict. It is also clear that the failure of the experiments intensified it still further. The Chinese were left with nothing but the revolutionary ideology to bolster their self-assurance and ambitions. But it could be used as an asset and turned to good political effect. In asserting that the Russians are now betraying the 'national liberation movements' in the way the social-democrats of the Second International betrayed 'proletarian internationalism', the Chinese were staking out their claim to world revolutionary leadership.

The underdeveloped countries—'the revolutionary centres of the world'—possessed a reservoir of revolutionary attitudes, based on nationalism and race feelings, which could be exploited. They are of course basically different from the ones on which Lenin naïvely pinned his hopes when he was denouncing the betrayal of internationalism by 'social reformists' and expected a revolution in Western Europe. But there is also a Leninist type of logic in the Chinese assertions that revolutionary opportunities should be exploited where they occur, and not in the countries where they should, but do not, occur. Chou En-lai expressed it very clearly in an interview given to a Western journalist (*New Statesman*, March 26, 1965):

> 'Being Marxist-Leninists, I have no need to tell you that we attach the greatest weight to the diffusion of revolutionary ideas among the workers' movement. But which are the first régimes to experience a revolutionary situation? Because a revolutionary situation must exist before the revolution can break out. Objectively, a revolutionary situation is produced above all in the backward regions. Marx and Engels did not foresee that the proletarian revolution would triumph in backward Russia. Lenin took a different view.'

The tables are thus neatly turned, and Lenin's logic applied in his time against the orthodox Western Marxists is now directed against the Soviet heirs of Lenin. The Soviet Marxist-Leninists are here in a quandary, the paradox of which they do not seem to appreciate.

Lenin stood Marx on his head and replaced his theory of revolution with his own voluntaristic version. To salvage the residual Marxist element in it he developed his theory of imperialism which transferred the emphasis in the analysis of revolutionary developments from their internal economic (or technological) dynamics to the international sphere. One of its logical corollaries was the expectation of the ultimately inevitable military clash of the socialist and capitalist worlds. But the explosion over Hiroshima necessitated the revision of this Leninist logic: the nuclear era required doctrinal adaptation in order to avoid the risk of being blown up. In short, metaphorically speaking, the atom barred the way to historical determinism. As a result, the Soviet Union and its leaders now find themselves precariously poised not only between China and the West, but also between the Marxist theory of revolution, which has been refuted by the experience of the Western industrial countries (where Marx and Lenin expected it), and the Leninist theory of imperialism, which is inapplicable in the nuclear age.

It is unlikely that the Russians will make any clear choice in the short run; they will probably go on trying to muddle through, avoiding the unpleasant alternatives of a capitulation to the Chinese doctrinal positions and the abandonment of the revolutionary claims of their régime. No ruling class will easily give up the position which justifies its right to rule. But in the long run it will probably be unable to avoid the transformation of the régime through which it rules into something far less dogmatic about its chiliastic future.

China may cling much longer to her fundamentalist dogmas, but she realizes the nuclear perils better than the Russians implied in the Sino-Soviet ideological dispute. And in the long run, as the technological gap between the technically advanced and the backward nations tends to grow rather than diminish, China may well have to make some agonizing choices when it reaches real nuclear status, i.e. when it has to try to carry the increasing burden of the nuclear arms race with perfected systems of delivery.

Yet even before that stage is reached, if it is reached, the Chinese may realize that, as Reinhold Niebuhr put it, 'the dogma promised a new heaven on earth, yet a nuclear encounter would annul all bourgeois and communist dreams in a final catastrophe'. And that goes for communists of both the 'dogmatic' and the 'revisionist' variety.

London,
June 1965

I
The Three Internationals

SPEAKERS

Jane Degras

Harry T. Willetts

Leopold Labedz

1. The Three Internationals

LABEDZ: 1964 marks the centenary of the foundation of the First International. So this is perhaps a fitting occasion to discuss the experiences of a movement which is theoretically based on internationalism, and to consider how its ideals have worked out in practice.

It is more than a hundred years since the *Communist Manifesto* proclaimed: 'Workers of all countries, unite!' This was in 1848. In 1960 a Soviet textbook on ideology, *The Fundamentals of Marxism-Leninism*, still asserted that 'during the past one hundred years the international solidarity and unity of the proletariat have considerably increased'. It claimed that 'this has found its expression primarily in the organization of the working-class movement'.

How *in fact* has the organization of the working-class movement, which is said to be embodied in the separate national parties, been expressed in political practice? Perhaps we should start with the First International, and see how the problem of combining the principle of internationalism with the interests of separate parties worked out in this case.

DEGRAS: I think the difficulty of combining the internationalist principle with the interests of the various national parties only became clear when the testing time came. And for the First International—indeed for the Second and Third too—the test came in wartime. The First International broke down after the Franco-Prussian war of 1870–71, although it survived for a little while and in fact held one congress after that war. The behaviour of the French and the German proletariat did not bear out the principles which Marx and the other founders of the First International had embodied in their charter and articles of association.

LABEDZ: Although it is true that the First International broke down in 1872, the strains and stresses were already visible before the Franco-Prussian war. They sprang, largely at least, from the conflicting ambitions of the two main tendencies within the International, the one headed by Marx and the other by Bakunin.

DEGRAS: The latter, the Anarchist Alliance, becoming affiliated against the protest of Marx and Engels!

17

LABEDZ: In fact the split occurred when, according to the best historical evidence at our disposal, Marx was in a minority. So the question how to handle an 'arithmetical majority' came up very early in the history of the movement.

WILLETTS: If we are considering the First International as an attempt to give international unity to a working-class movement, I think we must consider it in two aspects. First of all, we must consider it as an association of parties of the proletariat. Now, of course, most of these parties were embryonic and some of them were notional. The attempt to popularize the ideals of the International was accompanied by efforts to secure some sort of a united working-class action in practical matters. In fact, the ostensible reason for the formation of the First International was that it would make possible international action, for instance against attempts at strike-breaking by employers resorting to the import of foreign labour. If one looks at the report of the International for the year 1866, one finds that its greatest success was in dissuading the Belgians imported to break the Bermondsey basket-makers' strike from doing so. The Belgians were given their fare home by the International and went away and the strike continued.

There was some activity at this level, but even this, despite some minor successes, aroused very little interest among proletarian organizations, such as they were, in western Europe. From the point of view of Marx, the International was essentially a vehicle for the propagation of socialist ideas. So one has a second level: the ideological level. This is the level at which the kind of clash you have mentioned becomes serious.

LABEDZ: Perhaps it would be true to say in general that the maintenance of unity is harder in parties that are based on a community of opinion, of doctrine, than in those founded simply on shared interests. All the Internationals seem to have shown a tendency towards what the Chinese now call 'splittism', that is a divisive tendency aggravated by different ideological interpretations of the basic texts. In considering the causes of these divisive activities, one ought to look at two further elements: the struggle for power, and the problem of national identification. I think one can see fairly clearly the role these two elements were already playing even in the First International. I have here an excerpt from a letter by Marx to Engels, written in July 1869—that is, before the Franco-Prussian war—in which he says: 'This Russian (Bakunin) apparently wants to become the dictator of the European working-class movement. Let him take care, otherwise he will be officially excommunicated.' How familiar this language is! Perhaps it is worth recalling now in 1964 that this interaction between socialist ideology, nationalism and even personal power-struggles finds its precedent in the First International in the rivalry between Marx and Bakunin, who disliked Marx and called him a German Jew. Engels, writing to Marx less than a year later, expressed his horror about the idea that the European proletariat should achieve its unity 'under Russian command'. He said: 'Much as Bakunin exaggerates, it is obvious that this danger actually exists.'

As Willetts mentioned, the working class itself was not keen on importing foreign labour. This was not just on the occasion of this or that strike, but it was a consistent tendency on the part of workers in all the industrialized countries, including France and England. The question is whether there was in fact from the beginning any reason to anticipate anything else, to believe that the drawing into national life of the lower classes, proletariat and peasantry, and making the principle of citizenship more embracing, would result in greater internationalism.

WILLETTS: Going back to Marx and his 'nationalism', I am inclined to doubt whether there was really a national basis to his political prejudice. Marx was a western European; he believed that the proletarian revolution must begin from western Europe, and must be led by western Europeans. However, his reason for disliking and distrusting Russian revolutionary leaders was the backwardness of Russia, whom he could not see as a logical leader of an international working-class movement. Of course, he also strongly objected to the anarchist ideas which he associated with Russian revolutionary leaders at this stage. But I do not know whether this can really be termed a dispute of nationalist origin in the same sense as certain later disputes within the international socialist movement.

LABEDZ: In the nineteenth century nationalism was connected with liberal ideas. In the twentieth century, it came to be associated with radicalism either of the left or of the right, and it became violent and chauvinistic.

WILLETTS: Marx in particular was very ready, when he was abusing somebody, to invoke well-known characteristics of particular nationalities as part of his abuse. However, I do not think his attitude to people was basically conditioned by their nationality, or by their cultural background.

DEGRAS: In fact, you can find a good deal in the later writings of

Marx and Engels which pays high tribute to the Russian character, to the Russian revolutionaries, and to the organizations which they were beginning to found.

LABEDZ: Nevertheless Marx and Engels, particularly in private letters, were often ready to describe Russians, or Jews, or the French, or the English, or the Germans, for that matter, in scathing terms, abusing them for their real or alleged national characteristics.

WILLETTS: But isn't this all too human? Aren't we in the heat of battle—wrongly of course—all inclined to generalize and talk in this manner?

LABEDZ: Moving now to the causes of friction and to the causes of the eventual split in the Second International, here I think is a clear illustration of Jane Degras' point—the connection between the war and the difficulty in maintaining the international organization.

A year before the First World War, in 1913, the Second International adopted a resolution at its meeting in Basle opposing war and threatening unified action should a war occur. In fact, no such action took place and this was often mentioned later by Lenin as the cause of the breakdown of the Second International, and as the grounds for the creation of a new, Third International, based on real proletarian internationalism.

DEGRAS: But it was not merely the breakdown of the Second International that led to the creation of the Third. Primarily, I would say, the creation of the Third International was the outcome of an illusion on the part of the bolsheviks—shared by various prominent leaders in the West; for example, Lloyd George and Clemenceau—that a workers' revolution might possibly break out in western Europe as it had broken out in Russia. Lenin and the other bolshevik leaders believed that the masses of the workers were in fact ready to undertake a revolution of this kind, but were being held back by their social-democratic, reformist, social-patriotic leaders, as they called them. By supplying a new and revolutionary leadership, by creating a Third International based on the principles on which their own bolshevik revolution had been carried out, Lenin and his friends hoped to give leadership to the masses of France, Germany, Italy, perhaps even England, which would carry the revolution further. For they believed, as many others did, that the revolution in Russia was only the beginning of world revolution. To make the transition from the Russian to world revolution, they believed that all that was necessary was to provide revolutionary leadership for the proletariat, who were ready for it, but were not being led towards it by their old pre-1914 leaders. Lenin said that the Second International had broken down in 1914. He was referring primarily to the voting of war credits in the German Reichstag, because the criterion by which a party supported or did not support the military policy of its government was whether it voted for the war budgets, and the German Social Democratic Party did, in fact, with one or two exceptions, vote for the war budgets.

WILLETTS: It has always seemed extraordinary to me that somebody with such a keen sense of reality as Lenin should have seriously put forward the theory of a betrayal of the working-class by their leaders in 1914. If one looks at the history of the Second International what one sees, again, is a certain artificiality in the whole thing. On the one hand, there are international congresses where leaders of working-class parties pledge themselves to particular forms of international action and also, on many occasions, to certain general principles of political activity within their own countries. However, often enough the parties in question are not only ignorant of the principles which their leaders internationally profess, but certainly would not approve of those principles if they understood them. Indeed, one sees constant contradictions between the behaviour of these parties at home and their international professions.

Also, before the First World War, it was always clear that there were important differences of opinion within the leadership of the International on international questions. It was quite obvious that many of the German leaders had reservations about the way in which a war might be prevented by international working-class action. There were differences of opinion on the colonial question too: the delegates from the Low Countries, for instance, on occasions expressed themselves in favour of colonialism, on the ground that this would help to extend socialism to backward areas through the actions of European socialist movements. There were other contradictions of this kind, but of course the outstanding thing to remember about the Second International is that the mass membership of the European working-class parties did not know about its international obligations, and would not have accepted them. If they had acted to try to prevent war, the German social democrats and the French social democrats, for instance, would simply have cut themselves off from the masses. Presumably it was largely for this reason that they did not live up to their international obligations. In fact, they were aware that in this sort of crisis nationalism must triumph over internationalism and they adjusted themselves to the situation.

LABEDZ: In the historical experience of the international communist movement proper, that is, after the emergence of the Third International in 1919, I think we once again witness the same divergence between ideological professions and current political reality.

After the Second World War Leon Blum once referred to the French Communist Party as the 'foreign nationalist party'. I think that rather neatly summarized the subordination of the policies of the various communist parties to the changing exigencies of Soviet foreign policy. Until the split with Yugoslavia, or with China, it might have been believed by the communists that this was necessitated by the isolation of the Soviet Union, who accordingly required the unconditional support of all communist parties. Now I think it is clear to everybody that the situation changes where there is more than one communist ruling party. In fact it is not only in relations between bourgeois states that the principle of internationalism fails. It works no better amongst countries where the communist party is in power.

Can one detect anything of this development, which has become so conspicuous in our own day, back in the inter-war period?

DEGRAS: I think one can. Theoretically the difficulty was always overcome by reference to the simple slogan: 'Everything that is good for the Soviet Union is good for the international working class. Therefore there can be no divergence of interest between the two.'

On the other hand, the possibility of divergence was often implicitly admitted; never in so many words, of course, but in action. In Germany, for example, you had on two occasions the phenomenon of the trend in the communist movement which became known as 'national bolshevism', both in the early 'twenties and in the early 'thirties. Now the Russians realized that the nationalist parties in Germany had won a good deal of support by their advocacy of national aims, their opposition to the ratification of the Versailles Treaty and suchlike. You can find many resolutions and decisions of the Comintern stating in so many words that it was dangerous to overlook the national factor, and that it was wrong to allow the nationalist right-wing parties to be the only profiteers from nationalist feelings.

As for a definite divergence of interests between the Soviet state and a local party, take the Turkish Communist Party in 1920–21. It was being severely persecuted by the Turkish government, but the Turkish government itself was on excellent terms with the Soviet government. The Russians in fact sent the Turks military advisers and military assistance in their war with the Greeks, although they were perfectly aware—and this was made clear at congresses of the Comintern—that the same Turkish government was cruelly suppressing its own communists.

LABEDZ: You mentioned before that the practice of the Third International was based on the illusion—held not only by the communists —that western Europe was ripe for revolution, and that this would spread towards the Atlantic.

Even at this early stage there was, I think, a tendency already apparent to identify internationalism, not just with certain abstract principles, but with a particular national group, or with a particular geographical location. In the first issue of *Communist International* Lenin wrote that, for a time, the leadership of 'the proletarian International has passed to the Russians in the same way as at various periods in the nineteenth century it was enjoyed by the English, then by the French, and then by the Germans.' Here we have a sort of relay theory of the International; in fact, this theory was recently adopted by the Chinese and it stands to reason that if this international relay race goes on, the Chinese can take over the baton from the Russians, someone else from the Chinese and so forth—who shall say where this dialectical progression is to stop?

WILLETTS: Of course, one could argue that for the true internationalist it does not really matter where the world revolution begins, where the headquarters may temporarily be.

DEGRAS: In fact, Lenin said he would have preferred it in Berlin rather than in Moscow.

WILLETTS: And one might remember Marx's famous statement that a peasant revolution in Russia might give the stimulus for the outbreak of revolutions in Europe, which would later become socialist revolutions and make possible an international socialist state.

LABEDZ: But that was only one part of Marx's attitude. The other was determined by his ideas about the degree of industrialization that is needed to prepare the ground for the socialist revolution.

I think Marx would be very surprised to see that the relay race was going to be eastwards rather than westwards. He was a west European, and would surely have been amazed if he could have glimpsed the international staff of his socialist revolution operating in Peking while his proletarian revolution in Europe was as far round the corner as ever.

23

DEGRAS: Lenin certainly was aware of the possibility of a shift east-wards in the centre of revolution. He, for one, did not expect the concept of revolution to remain static.

LABEDZ: The concept of revolution may not remain static, but if it is not to be diluted to a degree where it would be impossible to call it Marxist, it must have a certain residuum of Marxist ideas.

Industrial structure is, for example, a precondition for the establish-ment of the dictatorship of the proletariat. But the more time passes, and the further eastwards or southwards we move, the smaller the chance of encountering and overthrowing an industrial structure and of establishing the dictatorship of a class which, without it, cannot exist.

DEGRAS: Yet, as Marx said, the class nature of a policy is defined by the policy itself, and not by the people who lead it. Trotsky echoed this after him, in connection with the Chinese revolution.

LABEDZ: That is so, but we can reduce this to a point where it is absurd. We can have a New Guinea or Borneo tribe exercising the dictatorship of the proletariat if they happen to have sent a few of their members to study in a developed country. If after their return they seize power and establish a 'People's Republic', this by some obscure process would then embody the dictatorship of the proletariat among the head-hunters!

After the Second World War our problem acquired a new dimen-sion. We have now to deal with the compatibility of interests, not just between parties, but between the states in which these parties operate and exercise power.

WILLETTS: In the case of several of the parties which achieved power after the Second World War, the problem was simplified by the fact that they could not have taken power, or at least not have retained power, without Soviet support. They were clients of the Soviet Union, and to that extent they were not a problem. Their own internal posi-tion made it necessary for them to accept Soviet tutelage and the extension of Soviet security arrangements into their own territory.

One exception among the ruling communist parties of eastern Europe was, of course, the Yugoslav Party which managed to prove that it was not so completely dependent as the others.

The position did not change in quite the same way for the parties completely outside the Soviet sphere. For instance, one would have thought that the Italian and French Communist Parties, which were

24

greatly strengthened as a result of the Second World War, might have found it possible to exercise a little more independence. Why did they not do so?

LABEDZ: I think that one can risk a generalization here. Strains in the relations with the Soviet Union first developed in those parties which were most successful in their independent struggle for power. This applies as much to Yugoslavia and to Albania as to China. The history of these countries' independence, such as it was, might have been ideologically fortuitous—it might have resulted largely from geographical isolation from the Soviet Union, as with Yugoslavia, or China, or Cuba. But all these parties also had experience of independent action, a cohesion between party cadres and leadership developed in their struggles, and all these factors created the loyalties, the homogeneity and identification of interests which, in turn, led to the crystallization of a position independent of the Soviet will. Ultimately it may clash with it.

WILLETTS: I would not quite agree with that. I would rather say that independent action has been *more* successful in those countries which established communist rule wholly or mainly by their own efforts; but this has not ruled out movements towards independence from Moscow in countries where Moscow was really, though not nominally, the dominant power.

LABEDZ: The criterion is surely the kind of identification which the party has; whether it identifies itself with the Soviet leadership, or with its own leadership. We know that after the war, to take one example, the French Party identified itself with the Soviet Union.
This was not the case in Yugoslavia after the split. Curiously enough, before the split, the Yugoslavs were probably the most eager of all the east European parties to identify themselves with the Soviet Union. The Soviet myth was still very strong at that time. However, since the expulsion of the Yugoslavs from Cominform, and with the process of fragmentation going on, the effectiveness of the myth in tying up the various parties with one single centre has diminished. It is a new situation when party cadres and the rank and file do not owe their first allegiance to Stalin or Khrushchev, but to Tito, or Mao, or Gomulka, or Gheorghiu Dej.

WILLETTS: Of course, we must take into account, in the case of each party, what gives that party its dynamic, its cohesion. In the case of Yugoslavia, it was obviously a national upsurge. There was a genuine national resistance movement against the Germans. In a sense it was a historical accident that that nationalist movement was organized and taken over by the Communist Party.

DEGRAS: In China, too, the dynamic of the Communist Party and of the establishment of the Chinese Communist State in 1949 was essentially a nationalist one. In fact, I should think it was more nationalist than any other revolutionary movement anywhere. And the French Communist Party, for instance, really began to make headway only when it presented itself as the most patriotic, the most 'French' party, in face of the German danger. When they called for the abrogation of the Versailles treaty, or for autonomy for Alsace-Lorraine, they got nowhere.

LABEDZ: The communists were, generally speaking, only successful in those countries where they succeeded in capturing local nationalism, where they could present themselves as patriots. The fact is that they could ride this nationalist horse in every country. Nevertheless the explanation of the Sino-Soviet split by old-China or old-Russia hands, leaves much to be desired. The fissiparous tendency is universal.

If we take a bird's eye view of the history of the last hundred years, and of all the attempts to harmonize the interests and the activities of socialist and then of the communist parties, we see typical contradictions recurring again and again despite the diverse histories and cultures of the various countries. It may be Marx versus Bakunin, Lenin versus Kautsky, Stalin versus Tito, Khrushchev versus Mao; it may be China, it may be Yugoslavia; it may hasten the split or defer it; but sooner or later the split comes, for it is impossible in the long run to reconcile national and power considerations in the struggle for 'socialism' with the mystique of internationalism. That can be the only explanation for the repeated failures of these internationalist hopes and professions of faith; there is more to it than just hypocrisy.

In Yugoslavia in 1948, when Tito and Kardelj were exchanging letters with comrades from the Russian Politburo, they said: 'Our only desire is to eliminate every doubt and disbelief in the purity of the comradely and brotherly feeling of loyalty of our Central Committee of the Communist Party of Yugoslavia to the Communist Party of the Soviet Union.'

Eleven years later, in Albania, two years before the split with Russia came to the surface, Enver Hoxha said in his speech in February 1959: 'The words of Comrade Khrushchev at the 21st Congress of the Communist Party of the Soviet Union express the genuine essence of proletarian internationalism.' Then he went on to say that friendship with the Soviet Union 'will live through the ages, like the majestic mountains of our Fatherland'.

DEGRAS: I do not think these statements should be taken at all seriously.

LABEDZ: Nor do I, of course—but how striking the ritual, the need for a liturgic repetition! It was the same in 1950, when Mao Tse-tung said: 'Everyone can see that the unity of the great Chinese and Soviet peoples, reinforced by a treaty, is lasting, durable and unshakable.' And all this unshakable unity falls to pieces in no time. Now, I do not think people like Mao are just hypocritical in the traditional, diplomatic sense. There is, of course, a good deal of hypocrisy here, but there is also an element of ideological befuddlement. There is no sober realization of the character of the process as we see it detachedly from outside. Ideological preconceptions provide the framework for both misconceptions and hypocrisy.

DEGRAS: But I think this kind of conventional invocation has its parallel under every régime—for example where parliaments are opened with a traditional form of words.

LABEDZ: But why do communist régimes have to bring in this particular sacred cow of internationalism? In an alliance which is based on a community of interests, even a temporary community of interests, we do not have to invoke first principles. Simple political necessity is an adequate justification for action.

WILLETTS: We must remember that we are dealing not with any sort of a genuine International, but with a system of alliances which was, when it was formed, based on a certain community of interests.

In the case of the east European countries, the community of interests is that of a number of régimes who depend on the Soviet Union for their survival.

DEGRAS: Nobody has attempted to form an International since the end of the Second World War.

LABEDZ: Well, they tried, with Cominform.

DEGRAS: That in fact was an alliance of the countries in the Soviet bloc, with the addition of the French and Italian Parties, which were not in power.

LABEDZ: I think that the concept of alliance has certain connotations which are misleading if it is applied to the relations between different communist parties, even after the Second World War. It would be certainly misleading if it were applied to situations existing before the Second World War. An ordinary alliance of states does not need ideological cement. Certainly nobody in an alliance invokes the principle of 'internationalism'. The two things are incompatible. Either you have internationalism, and then you do not need an alliance, or you have an alliance, and then you do not have to invoke the principle of internationalism.

DEGRAS: Of course, we could go back to the definition of internationalism put out by the Comintern in the 'thirties.

WILLETTS: I think we should, because I think we would find that in Sino-Soviet relations, for instance, since the establishment of the Chinese People's Republic, there is no vestige of true internationalism in any traditional Marxist sense. Internationalism is supposed to involve, amongst other things, sacrifices, an international community of labour. The Soviet Union never looked like giving aid to China on a scale approaching what a traditional Marxist would have considered to be its duty to give. At no time was there a greater co-ordination of policies than you get between any two normal allies. Relations between Britain and the United States, for instance, were probably at all stages closer in this sense than those between the Soviet Union and China.

LABEDZ: Precisely, and that is why I think we have to explain this seeming paradox, that the countries which profess common attachment to one single principle, namely proletarian internationalism, find that this is not a cementing but a divisive factor, and that it eventually obstructs rather than helps in the co-ordination of policy.

WILLETTS: They are stuck with an obsolete ideology. But surely this is no more difficult to understand than their claim that their system is supported by the whole population of their countries.

LABEDZ: I certainly agree that this is an obsolete ideology, but I do not think that the matter can be explained away simply by saying that the Soviet bloc is another form of the traditional system of alliances.

28

DEGRAS: I would agree with Willetts that the appeals to proletarian internationalism are traditional invocations to which nobody attaches any meaning.

LABEDZ: Well, I myself do not. We know very well that one can invoke the principle of internationalism for the sake of the most narrow or chauvinistic interests. But even if we stand outside the 'theology' of communism, as it were, we cannot understand the internal struggle or the character of its rationalizations if we try and reduce the whole process to meaninglessness. And that is what we should be doing if we said that the bloc was nothing but the traditional sort of alliance. We know in fact that it is not an alliance: we know that there are clashes of interest which cannot be resolved by pragmatic compromise, and we know that both sides have to justify not only their internal but also their international behaviour by holy scripture.

How could one explain in purely 'alliance' terms a situation where a movement which was born in Germany, tutored in England and had its philosophy formulated for it in terms of the Hegelian dialectic by Marx, is now experiencing a 'theological' battle in which the Deputy Director of the Chinese Central Committee's propaganda department, Chou Yang, can get up and invoke the principle of the dialectic to explain the Sino-Soviet rift? On the face of it, there is something here that must be explained. It is not like a situation of, say, the alternating *rapprochement* and cooling-off between France and the United States. The Sino-Soviet quarrel is a different kind of process.

WILLETTS: The two parties share the same myth, which is one of the instruments of rule for each of them.

LABEDZ: It is becoming a myth of many skins. First it was internationalism and the proletariat; then nationalism and the peasantry; now, perhaps, it may be colour and underdevelopment.

What explains the necessity to keep up the myth?

WILLETTS: Both parties are committed to the idea of eventual world unification, in the same way as both are committed to the idea of an eventual stateless society, but I am not convinced that one means more than the other.

LABEDZ: Do you think there is any chance that one of the parties, specifically the Soviet Party, is likely to give up the myth, because, as you said, the ideology is obsolete, and may in some cases be an obstacle to the realization of one's own interests?

DEGRAS: I do not think they will give it up, but I think the myth itself, as so many myths do, will gradually fade away.

LABEDZ: How is it likely to affect Sino-Soviet relations?

WILLETTS: I should have thought the development of their state relations was to some extent independent of the myth. After all, the Yugoslavs and the Russians have not settled all their ideological differences by any means, but they have a kind of working agreement for certain purposes. Is it unthinkable that something similar should happen with the Soviet Union and China?

LABEDZ: It is quite thinkable. Only the problem is now different. Politically Yugoslavia needed merely to survive, whereas with China it is a struggle for hegemony.

DEGRAS: Yugoslavia nevertheless tried to get allies on its own side, against Moscow.

LABEDZ: True, but Yugoslavia was not in fact offering itself as a model and Tito did not aspire to become the supreme interpreter of the faith.

DEGRAS: It was not big, or powerful, enough to do so.

LABEDZ: It was not, therefore, trying to build its own following on an international scale, as the Chinese are.

DEGRAS: Yes, they are big and that is the crucial factor.

LABEDZ: And on this, I think, we all agree.

2

The Split
in the Open

SPEAKERS

Brian Crozier

Roderick MacFarquhar

Leopold Labedz

2. The Split in the Open

LABEDZ: The Sino-Soviet dispute is now in the open and it is clear that it has created a fundamentally new situation in the world. We can no longer talk of *one* eastern or communist bloc and, since General de Gaulle's initiative to take up diplomatic relations with China, the western pole of the now defunct bi-polarity has also shown signs of no longer being the single magnet it was at the time of Stalin and the heyday of NATO. But while, to use the words of Lenin, the western democracies can be relied upon to patch up their differences through 'unprincipled compromise', the rift between the two contending centres of communist thinking and, increasingly, power, would appear to be a very different affair.

CROZIER: It seems to me that there are two aspects to the dispute: one is ideological, the other is a matter of a clash between two great powers, or at least between one super-great power, and a very large country which has all the potentialities of being a great power, but perhaps has not yet reached the position to which she feels that history has beckoned her.

The Chinese, on the ideological side, are challenging the Russians for the leadership of the world communist movement. In effect they have named Mr. Khrushchev as the main obstacle to the progress of communism in the world. So long as Mr. Krushchev remains in power, or, alternatively, so long as the present Chinese leadership remains in power, it is impossible for any kind of reconciliation to take place.

As regards the great-power clash, it is a latent thing. As soon as the Chinese communists came to power in 1949, they announced that they were going to seek a revision of their frontiers, and specifically of the unequal treaties imposed on them by the imperial powers in the last century. Clearly the Russians were among these imperial powers, and it was only early this year [1964] that the Chinese mentioned, for the first time, the need to revise the treaties that had been imposed on China by Tsarist Russia. That, it seems to me, is the great-power angle.

MACFARQUHAR: We have witnessed here, I think, the end of the communist bloc in the form we have known it for a decade. Certain further steps could be taken, such as breaking off diplomatic relations or a conference to read China out of the communist bloc, but we have already witnessed the end. It seems to me this will have profound implications for the impact of communism on unconverted, uncommitted peoples, because the great magnetism of communism has been its ability to pose as the main wave of the future. When the wave has split into two smaller currents, when the leaders of the communist bloc are quarrelling and denouncing each other in the same tones that they denounce the 'imperialists', I cannot see any longer that people can be convinced that this is the united and unbeatable wave of the future. The second point is that from the purely Chinese point of view this marks the end, to some extent, of an attempt to absorb China into European or western civilization. China is still in the grip of a European ideology, Marxism, but she is no longer part of a European-led bloc or even a European cultural area. More and more, she is going to evolve her own combination of Marxism and the Chinese and Asian reality, and she will attempt to lead people herself and not accept the leadership of the Europeans. She has already, in her articles, been denouncing the Europeanization of Marxism and it seems to me that this trend will continue. The Russians on their part are deploring what they call 'the Sinification of Marxism'.

Crozier's division into ideological and great-power aspects of the rift is perhaps a little artificial: I think the ideology is merely the cloak for the great-power ambitions, under which I would include not just frontier revision, but also foreign policy. I would say that the importance of ideology has always been that once you state your point of view in ideological terms, you are to some extent taking up a position from which you cannot really retreat, because there can only be *one* person who decides on ideology within the communist bloc. If you state your position in ideological terms, you say: '*I* am the person who decides on ideology and I am going to take this line. Either you agree with me or you are not a Marxist.'

LABEDZ: Is the situation now comparable to the one which existed when the communist sects were struggling with each other but the parties were not yet in power? In other words, is there any possibility now that we will see a reunification of the communist movement on a world scale, with China taking over from Russia the lead of the unitary movement in the same way in which the bolsheviks, having split the socialist movement after the First World War, challenged the Second International and created the Third International, saying that *they* were fulfilling the revolutionary message of Marx in a *revolutionary* International? Does the situation warrant such an assumption, taking into account that we are no longer dealing with warring factions within one party, or even within one international movement which is aspiring to power, but with parties which are *in* power and which have at their disposal and under their control the means of power?

CROZIER: I think, in a way, you have answered your own question. Like all parallels, it is a tempting one. I think the great difference between now and the 1920s or 1930s is that in those days it was a question of one socialist state and a lot of parties that were not actually in power. So it was a relatively easy thing for the Soviet leaders, although admittedly they had their own internal disputes, to impose their views on the rest of the communist movement. Now the fundamental difference is that we have two very large communist states, each with world ambitions of its own. I think that the possibilities of reconciliation are much smaller than they were in the previous historical period of dissension.

MACFARQUHAR: By a similar token I think comparisons people sometimes make between the split in the West—between De Gaulle and the United States—and the split in the East—between Mao and Khrushchev—are rather far-fetched. De Gaulle may have delusions of grandeur; he may think that he can lead Europe, but practically no one else believes that France can be the leader, an alternative leader, of the West. America is the only foreseeable leader of the West in the next generation, whereas the Chinese, and the people to whom the Chinese appeal, can quite easily see China as not only an alternative leader, but eventually perhaps as *the* leader. I think I would agree with both of you: in my opinion there is no chance of a reunification under Chinese leadership.

LABEDZ: If there is no chance of reunification, then what are the political implications in terms of international relations, in terms of the international balance of power and in terms of the impact of the split on the various communist parties of the world?

MACFARQUHAR: My feeling is that for the Chinese the great thing at issue with the Russians has been the Russian failure to support Chinese foreign-policy aims, particularly the attempt to recover Formosa and the attempts to get the Americans out of the Far East. Since the Russians refused to help the Chinese, the fact that they are now no longer allies of the Chinese will make very little difference to the Chinese posture as against the Americans. So I do not think that the political implications for China will include any reversal of major foreign-policy postures. They will still attempt by every means in their power to get the Americans out of the Far East and to get Formosa back.

However, when one takes China's communist aims specifically—not foreign policy aims, though these are included— and when China says, as she has done in her dispute with the Russians, 'We must promote revolution', and the Russians have to some extent rejected this as being too dangerous, the Chinese, being relieved of the constraint of having to agree with the Russians for the sake of public unity, will now more and more attempt to drum up support in what is loosely called 'the third world'—Africa, Asia and Latin America—and in the communist parties of these countries. We have already seen Russian accusations that the Chinese are attempting to draw a colour bar in international communist front organizations against the Russians, who, they say, are white men, and should not be there. I do not think that the Chinese have colour prejudice in the normally accepted meaning of the term. I do not think that they really have any sense of colour, but they *will* attempt to use colour and to use poverty. They *will* say to the Africans, Asians and Latin-Americans: 'We are poor like you, we have an industrial revolution to complete. The Russians are a developed country, a white country, and they have nothing more to teach you.'

LABEDZ: Aren't we too ready to overdraw the differences between the communist have-s and the communist have-nots, between Russia and communist China, between potential wealth on the one hand and poverty on the other, with the Chinese still displaying the old, revolutionary tradition and the Russians being in the throes of *embourgeoisment*? Has the Russian accusation of Chinese racialism not been overdrawn? Has China's appeal to the underdeveloped countries been really as effective as this kind of identification would lead one to believe?

CROZIER: There are really two issues here: one is an economic issue and the other is a racial issue which is related to it.

On the economic issue, it seems to me that there is an absolutely fundamental divergence in that Russia is a country which is potentially much richer than China, certainly in the immediate future. It has, or thinks it has, a chance of overtaking the United States. Whether it can or not is another matter, but Mr. Khrushchev has publicly announced his intention of overtaking the United States. What are the main differences economically between Russia and China? Surely one of the fundamental points at issue is that the resources of the communist world as a whole were not being used in the way that the

Chinese wanted them to be used. In effect Khrushchev has said: 'We are an advanced country. We have to demonstrate that our system is better than the capitalist system. We have a chance of doing that. Therefore we must use our resources in the way we think fit.' The Chinese have said in effect: 'Yes, but the essential thing is to help us develop, so that we catch up with the more advanced communist countries.' In 1956, after the Hungarian revolution, there was a dispute over the allocation of resources. The Chinese had backed the Russians over the intervention in Hungary. They expected some kind of return for it, instead of which the Russians diverted credits to the east European countries to help to still discontent there. Then again, in 1960, the Russians withdrew their technicians from China. So it comes down to a fundamental issue of poor countries and rich, and what is the best way of making use of available resources.

On the racial question, I agree with MacFarquhar; quite obviously the Chinese have been playing the racial issue, not necessarily because they believe in it, but because it makes an obvious appeal to the underdeveloped countries and that is clearly where the Chinese see the main field of battle between themselves and the Russians.

MACFARQUHAR: My comment on Labedz's original statement would be that the racial angle may well have been overplayed, and especially one may have overplayed the extent to which this will make an appeal in Africa and Asia. I think that we tend to underestimate the sophistication of people who are continually being bombarded with propaganda from all sides. It may have been overplayed, but nevertheless Chou En-lai was able to start his tour of black Africa with the memory of the Moscow racial riot (of December 1963) just behind him. This was perhaps just one thing that he could brandish in his hosts' face, but it was an important point. The more important issue is that China really has nothing as yet to offer but her words and her ideas. When Chou En-lai toured the Aswan Dam, it must have been a bitter pill to realize that no matter how much his words might carry conviction— and probably in Egypt they carried less than elsewhere—it is only the Russians and the Americans who can provide the money which all African, Asian, and Latin-American states want.

LABEDZ: What has been the Russian reaction, not in terms of ideological propaganda, but in political action?

CROZIER: The Russians face a dilemma. They have put a great deal of effort into Africa and so far they have had very little success. They have initiated all kinds of aid schemes, for instance, in Guinea, which seemed a natural thing for them to attempt because Guinea had been cut off without a penny by the French in 1958. These schemes have been a complete failure. President Sekou Touré, instead of thinking, 'At last I have found my place in the world', is trying to get back into the French orbit for economic reasons. For this reason, and for the reasons that MacFarquhar mentioned—the racial demonstration in Moscow in December 1963—it is rather difficult for the Russians to counter the kind of propaganda which the Chinese are putting out. Incidentally, on this point of racialism, one forgets perhaps that certain Guinean students did not feel at all happy at the treatment they received in Peking either. This, however, did not make as much splash as the riots in Moscow.

The Chinese have been trying to create a new kind of Afro-Asian movement which, they say, would be 'in the spirit of Bandung'. Of course one remembers that the Russians were excluded from Bandung in 1955, whereas the Chinese were present. The argument they put out is not simply that the Russians are white, but also that they are imperialists, and that the claim of the Soviet Union to be an Asian power is based on the imperialism of Tsarist Russia and therefore is a claim which cannot be admitted in an Afro-Asian movement. The Russians, although faced with the dilemma of how to get over this kind of propaganda, have considerable support within the Afro-Asian movement, for instance from the Indians. India has been invaded, or thinks she has been invaded, in part of her territory by China, and Russia has been 'neutral' on the Indian side.

LABEDZ: Do you think the Russian position has been fundamentally affected by this? I do not mean simply in terms of the propaganda battle, in front organizations or over the radio; I mean in the sense that, for the first time since the war, Russia has now not only to face the West, but also the East. That is, it has to reckon, in its foreign-policy considerations, not only with the balance of power as it exists between America and western Europe and the Soviet Union, but also in terms of its relations with China, and such potential customers as the Chinese may succeed in getting in the communist bloc.

MACFARQUHAR: I do not think anyone who has spoken to Russians about China can be unaware that there is some kind of a deep-seated psychological fear in a lot of Russians' minds about this vague menace that might appear from the East. This includes conversations that I had as far back as 1959, before the split was beginning to be at all obvious. However, I cannot believe that Khrushchev, or any immediate successor, formulating Russian foreign policy, would allow that foreign policy to be dictated by any consideration of a real threat from the East. I would think it more likely, as I suggested in the case of China, that Russia will be confirmed in her present foreign-policy positions. I take these to be to reach the kind of accommodations with the West which, while not giving anything vital away, will render the chances of war less likely, and at the same time courting people like Nasser and Nehru and the national bourgeoisie leaders of the 'third world' in an attempt to bring them over to the communist side, not, as the Chinese would seem to advocate, primarily through revolution, but through gradual diplomatic magnetism—tying them to the Russian side by aid and so on. As Crozier has pointed out, I think they have already found that this is not a sure-fire method. In fact, as the Americans have experienced, it often produces precisely the opposite results.

LABEDZ: How will the Russians' new and uncomfortable position of having to face two ways affect their fortunes in eastern Europe? Will the balance of power between China and Russia give the east European countries a greater margin of manœuvre? Will they be freer to resist Russian pressures and control?

CROZIER: It is a very paradoxical situation, is it not, because China has been the great denunciator of revisionism? Yet China's own action, by striking out on an individual line of her own, is in fact encouraging revisionism—revisionism in the sense of no longer blindly supporting Soviet orthodoxy. Even a year ago one would have said, if ever any party was really conformist and orthodox it was the Rumanian Party. Yet the Rumanians have been asserting themselves. They have been objecting to the division of labour proposed by Russia under Comecon.*

Then again, one has the paradox that the Chinese, although they condemned the Hungarian revolution, did side with Gomulka up to a point in 1956, at least to the extent of putting some pressure on Khrushchev not to intervene by force. So the Poles have recently tried to cast themselves as mediators between Peking and Moscow, not, as far as I am aware, with any success. The Chinese, by claiming to have a new orthodoxy, or to be the only real upholders of the old orthodoxy, are in fact encouraging other communist régimes to strike out on a line of their own.

* In April 1964 they came out with what almost amounted to a 'declaration of independence'; they sent a high-powered delegation to the United States which came back with valuable agreements; they broke away from bloc discipline at the (1964) Geneva Trade Conference; they made approaches to GATT, the International Monetary Fund and the World Bank.

LABEDZ: I am not sure that I would agree with attributing the present attempts at reconciliation on the part of the Polish Party to some sort of gratitude for 1956. I think their reasons are different.

CROZIER: I did not mean that they are making them for reasons of gratitude, but I meant that the Poles probably considered that they were *personæ gratæ* with the Chinese in a way that some of the other east European parties were not.

MACFARQUHAR: Any serious communist, and I take Gomulka to be such in the old style, must be worried at the prospect of the split. The kind of split which has occurred, and which could become even more public by open denunciations, diminishes the prestige of communism wherever it is. No communist power is an island and everything that detracts from communism in Russia, or communism in China, also affects the prestige of communism in Poland and throughout the world. My own feeling is that Gomulka is genuinely worried that a communist split will be bad for communism. I think also he may have a particular national worry and that is: so long as the powers are at odds, but not yet split, all the 'satellite' states have room for manœuvre. Once the split is open and irrevocable, the Russians no longer need to have the same diplomacy and finesse, perhaps, in soliciting the support of the 'satellites' because there is nothing to solicit their support on behalf of. They know that they will never be part of a Chinese-led, anti-Russian communist world movement. They might, as the Rumanians have done, have some freedom of manœuvre while the bloc is more or less in one piece, but once the bloc is irrevocably split I should imagine their chances of playing off one side against the other would be much reduced or nil.

LABEDZ: You may be attributing to the motivation of Gomulka's policy more sophistication than it really possesses. It has been said that he is the only man in Poland now who is still a true believer, and you may be right in saying that he takes his ideology seriously.

MACFARQUHAR: Not his ideology, but the prestige of communism. But I would like to suggest that this freedom of manœuvre which we have noticed cannot be completely ascribed to the split. I think it is true to say that the Hungarians have obtained a great deal more freedom internally since the revolution in 1956 than a number of other satellite countries. There has also been a general fermentation in these countries as a result of the Hungarian uprising, and the Russians are now very anxious to prevent any situation from arising which might again put them in the dilemma of either having to suppress a popular revolt by force or of condoning the secession of a member of their bloc. This has resulted in a greater amount of freedom for the individual communist leaders to attempt to run their countries as best they can, so that the parties may be made stronger and trouble may be avoided.

LABEDZ: What I am trying to elicit here is an explanation of a phenomenon which seems to me striking indeed. In 1956 we had two countries which moved a long way towards emancipation: Poland and Hungary. There were also some stirrings in Czechoslovakia, but Rumania remained silent. Today, however, Rumania, while remaining Stalinist, has moved at least towards a measure of economic self-determination. The Czechs, who remained Stalinist when Hungary erupted and Poland nearly erupted in violence, are moving out of the rut while resenting every penny they have to spend aiding under-developed countries. It is, paradoxically, the Gomulka régime, which faced considerable dangers in 1956, that now appears to be for a reconciliation between China and Russia though it is quite clear that the freedom of manœuvre which the 'satellites' enjoy depends—as you say—directly on the balance between the two communist super-powers. If this balance ceases to exist, there will be no room for manœuvre because the Russians will have no need to grant concessions.

CROZIER: It seems to me, too, that the present situation, which is a conflict, not perhaps the final split, works on the whole to the advantage of the east European countries. I am not sure that a complete reconciliation would be to their advantage, nor that a complete split would be. I should have thought there would be disadvantages in both.

MACFARQUHAR: They have at the moment the power of blackmail.

LABEDZ: Precisely, but then why should Gomulka take this position? One must remember that the communists in those ex-satellite countries which have attained a degree of autonomy face the problem of making their power legitimate in the eyes of the people. In the safe satellites this problem did not arise, because power there was simply a reflection of the Soviet Russian presence. In other words, the parties in question suffer intensely from the contrast between the doctrinal presumption that communism is the wave of the future, and the Sino-Soviet rift, which makes it clear to everyone who has eyes to see that the wave of the future is *not* the wave of the future, that history has no predetermined end, and that in fact what we have here is a conflict between two ideocratic countries who cloak their power-interests in an ideology.

MACFARQUHAR: But why Gomulka, not Kádár?

LABEDZ: Well, Kádár has chosen another way. In order to make himself more popular, he went further with internal liberalization; Gomulka has done precisely the opposite.

CROZIER: Gomulka, you might say, started off with a good dose of liberalization, but has gradually taken back the liberties that the Poles acquired in 1956.

MACFARQUHAR: Yes, but the greater the liberalization internally, the more reason, on your definition, to legitimize the power in real terms.

LABEDZ: I think that you face here a certain dilemma. You can choose between two possible roads. One road would be to use the deepening of the split to take further steps towards internal liberalization. If you do not choose this way and you tighten the screws, although you pretend to do something about the mutual abuse between the Russians and the Chinese, you really have in the end to fall in with the Russians.

That is precisely what Gomulka is doing; perhaps he has a small amount of support for this in the party hierarchy; but presumably everybody else in the country, outside the Party, would prefer the first road, that is, making things easier, and, incidentally, making therefore the Party more popular through liberalization.

CROZIER: It is not a question of real reconciliation, but of ensuring that the split does not widen irredeemably.

LABEDZ: Perhaps we may move a little geographically, from eastern Europe to the West, and consider what sort of impact the Sino-Soviet conflict is likely to have on the position of the West in general and the opportunities which are now open, or possibly will be open in the future, for western political initiative.

MACFARQUHAR: I said at the beginning that one of the major reasons of the dispute was that the Chinese found that the Russians were not supporting their major foreign policy objectives. I think, if we look at it from the American end, we will find that the American China policy, which many of us have criticized over the years, has in fact been one of the root causes of the dispute. It is a common thing to say: 'Nothing the West can do can make the dispute worse, or improve it'. It seems to me pretty obvious that it was the American China policy—a mere stalemate policy of standing still—which the Chinese were unable to do anything about by themselves, and for which they required Soviet help, that has been a major factor in the dispute, because the Russian help never came. We saw this very clearly in the 1958 Formosa Straits crisis. One of the implications for the West, for the Americans anyway at the moment, would be that they should probably maintain their present position on China. On the Russian side, they should take advantage of the Russian desire since the Cuban crisis in 1962 for limited accommodations, and move towards whatever arrangements can be made about nuclear weapons, surprise attack and so on.

CROZIER: You have been looking at the situation from the point of view of the great powers—on the communist side, of the parties actually in power. Perhaps one ought to say a word or two about the western communist parties, which really are in a very unhappy position. The West has its own ways of reaching affluence, and has been doing very well in terms of economic growth, so that communism does not make a fundamental appeal there. In the Sino-Soviet dispute, therefore, the western communist parties are bound to side with the Russians. Although we know that the Chinese have sent emissaries to the main western communist parties, and have tried to distribute propaganda to bring them round to their particular views, these have so far been of no more than nuisance value.

MACFARQUHAR: I would entirely agree with that. The communist parties of western Europe have pinned their faith for their future— particularly in Italy and in Britain—on the possibility of a peaceful transition to power. One of the things that the Chinese have constantly poured scorn on, if not rejected outright, has been the possibility of peaceful transition to power. It seems to me that no western communist party would want to abandon that general thesis and adopt the militant policies of the Chinese. The communist parties have difficulty enough getting electors in the West to vote for them. To adopt Chinese-type theses would be to commit electoral suicide.

LABEDZ: If I may draw conclusions from your two respective points of view—Crozier's being that there is no fundamental communist appeal on economic grounds to the populations of the western countries, and MacFarquhar's that the western communist parties pin their faith to peaceful transition—then the logical conclusion from these two premises taken together is that they have no chance of reaching power. Now, I should think that, being fairly large organizations with a certain historical, doctrinal and ideologically non-electoral tradition behind them, parties such as the French and Italian parties would try to avoid the horns of this particular dilemma. They want power, as do all political parties, and they will have to think of making a fresh appeal to the population if they want to stay in business. This situation will mark them off distinctly from other communist parties and I rather think that their common interests may eventually start a fresh polycentric development. Whether this will take the form of a regional grouping of parties or national types of communism, is too early to say. But it seems certain that by striking out on their own the Chinese have set in motion a process into which other communist parties are being increasingly drawn. They may now begin to look after their own interests without fear of excommunication or even of losing Russian support, and this is the new fact which communists everywhere may eventually be anxious to exploit. I can even imagine that a multiplication of centres may be presented as a respectable Marxist development, for it merely shows that societies and economies which are as vastly different from each other as are those of Russia, Italy and China, need a different kind of party and a different programme to help them along the pre-ordained routes of history towards its appointed goal. But what, if anything, remains of the world movement if each party is given its head and is determined to use it, is another matter.

44

3

The Sino-Soviet Conflict and Eastern Europe

SPEAKERS

William E. Griffith

Deryck Viney

Leopold Labedz

3. The Sino-Soviet Conflict and Eastern Europe

LABEDZ: Before the last war, eastern Europe used to be a hotbed of nationalist ambitions and antipathies. After the war, the communist régimes established there proclaimed an end to this era. But did they in fact put an end to it? Have the ancient nationalisms of eastern Europe been modified to any real extent by the social and political changes of the period? In all the eight countries of the region communist parties are in power. So the question arises at two different levels: at the level of communist parties and their relationship within the international communist movement, and at the level of governments, of state relations within the communist bloc.

GRIFFITH: One must begin by appreciating the world-wide strength of nationalism today. Ours is *the* era of nationalism. Even in western Europe, where the talk of, and indeed the considerable progress toward, European integration has made many people imagine that nationalism is on the decline, the opposite example of de Gaulle's France has proved that this is not so. And the cases of Cuba, Panama, indeed the United States itself, suggest the same for the New World. As for eastern Europe, nationalism there was suppressed during the Stalinist period; and nationalism suppressed is always nationalism redoubled. Khrushchev's aim was to reorganize eastern Europe on lines more like a commonwealth than an empire; this gave a certain leeway to nationalism and probably succeeded only in further intensifying it. And the latest example we have had of a partial, but successful, defiance of the Soviet Union—Rumania's—merely shows once more that in every part of the world nationalism remains, and increasingly represents, the primary political factor of our time.

LABEDZ: Has the Sino-Soviet conflict any role to play here? Has the aggravation of state relations and party relations between Peking and Moscow any appreciable effect on the communist régimes of eastern Europe?

VINEY: Certainly—though the Sino-Soviet issue only arose when the increase in nationalism, noticeable since Stalin's death, was already well advanced.

I would not agree that nationalism is the *primary* political factor everywhere today—is it in West Germany, for example?—but certainly in east Europe, where national pride has so often in history been the condition for survival, and where it has so often been affronted, it has again become the channel through which every public aspiration or resentment tends increasingly to flow. The channel has always been there, but now the floodgates have been lifted. Khrushchev gave the handle a first turn, as Griffith says, hoping to profit from the drop in internal pressure; but in Poland and Hungary the rushing waters proved nearly uncontrollable.

Khrushchev just managed to keep his empire together. But after 1956, régimes like those of Gomulka, Kádár or Dej, however loyal to Moscow, were more inclined and more able to press their own national interests, as they saw them, in cases where they diverged from Moscow's. Then, finally, along came the Sino-Soviet dispute to strengthen their hand, so that now it is the Rumanian leaders themselves, for example, who when it suits them turn the winches and allow the nationalist water-level to rise, sure of gaining popularity when it does.

Not, of course, that Peking preaches nationalism as such; she could no more afford to inflame racial minorities within her borders than Moscow could. But the very story of the dispute and its origins— backward China being refused economic and technical assistance by Big Brother, and so having to reappraise her relations, fend for herself, trade with the West however wicked—all this was welcome material for nationalist sermons. But still more important was the breakdown in the monolithic system of authority, as a result of which any satellite leader, Stalinist or revisionist, can now wield the threat of turning to the other side—or, like Ulbricht perhaps, gain kudos merely by refusing to wield it!

But the arch-wielders of course have been the Rumanians. Comecon would have practically limited their heavy industry to chemicals. Dej, like Mao, wanted to be more autonomous. How convenient for him when the dispute with China blew up to such dimensions within the communist world that the Rumanians could declare themselves neutral in that matter, at the same time criticizing Comecon's whole *raison d'être* and insisting on the equal rights of all communist parties— 'there can be no parent party'. Meanwhile Bucharest has maintained relations with Albania, reached economic agreements with America, signed a technical and trade pact with China, embarked on a *rapprochement* with Gaullist France—and Moscow, far from protesting, feels it wiser to comment less and less for fear of making matters worse and worse.

LABEDZ: Historically, of course, the first case of a successful revolt against the domination of Moscow was that of the Yugoslavs, a long time before the Sino-Soviet conflict. Later, the Yugoslav issue became entangled with the larger Sino-Soviet one. But let us cast our minds back and consider how nationalism and ideology entered into Soviet-Yugoslav relations, first, after Stalin had pronounced his anathema against Belgrade in 1948, and secondly, when Mao pronounced *his* in 1957.

GRIFFITH: If we take the first break between Moscow and Belgrade, back in 1948, then clearly nationalism rather than ideology was the prime factor. For the Yugoslavs were not reformist or 'revisionist' at all; ever since 1945 their Party had been one of the most leftist, if you will, of any. But Stalin insisted on seeking complete and direct control of the Yugloslav Party, armed forces and secret police. This was too much for Tito and so he became, perforce, a 'deviationist' in Moscow's eyes; but how reluctant a deviationist he was became clear from the eagerness with which he welcomed Khrushchev's moves toward a *rapprochement* in the years following Stalin's death. He hoped, first, to re-enter the international communist family of which he considered himself a legitimate member, but, secondly, to increase in the process his own influence in eastern Europe, especially in the Balkans.

In the second Soviet-Yugoslav break—the one that came after the Polish October and the Hungarian Revolution of 1956—not only were the Yugoslavs once more reluctant agents, but the Soviets themselves were hardly less so. The most recent Chinese revelations seem to me to confirm what we should all have seen clearly from the start: that the prime mover in that case was Mao, with Khrushchev tagging along behind.

The second break was followed by a second *rapprochement*, from 1960 on, and since then Soviet-Yugoslav relations have improved apace, in inverse proportion as Soviet-Chinese relations have deteriorated. The question of nationalism, of course, has now acquired a special importance for Yugoslavia; for the growing tension between the various nationalities *within* her border, as Tito ages and the succession problem looms, made the Yugoslavs more anxious than ever to come to terms with Moscow.

LABEDZ: Yes, and of course there are other reasons too—such as Chinese hostility to Tito and patronage of Albania next door. . . . But since we are speaking of Yugoslavia and China, I am reminded of the irritation evinced by the Yugoslav press during Chou En-lai's tour of

Africa over Chinese attempts to promote a second Bandung Conference of Afro-Asian states. . . .*

GRIFFITH: . . . from which, of course, the Yugoslavs, and the Russians too, would be excluded as Europeans, in contrast to the 1958 Belgrade Conference of Non-aligned Nations where the Yugoslavs revelled in their triple role as hosts, neutralists and representatives of Europe! As a countermove they are promoting a second Belgrade Conference of Non-aligned States. But of course Yugoslavia's special desire to cut a figure among the underdeveloped countries, especially in Africa and Asia, goes back a long way.

VINEY: Yes, we could see this policy beginning to develop quite soon after the Cominform break with Belgrade. The Yugoslavs realized that if they were out of the communist camp, yet at the same time could not properly join the western camp, they must see if there was any other area where they could throw their weight in—and about. After all any country which is small, yet aspires to a major international role, must seek a field of activity where smallness does not matter so much. And it was amongst these underdeveloped countries, non-aligned as between East and West, that Yugoslavia as a country within Europe and on the fringe of the communist camp could aspire to such a role. She could hope to increase her weight on the international scene by voicing the ambitions of some of the underdeveloped countries, and by giving them the benefit of her own advice on how to play off East against West.

After the Cominform break, another reason for Belgrade's interest in the 'third force' area was to try and exploit her standing amongst them by lining some of them up on her own side in her dispute with Moscow, or perhaps by threatening to stir them up against Moscow's policies, as she is indeed believed to have done at certain times in Egypt. Later Belgrade acquired a further interest in exploiting her

* In August 1964, when the Soviet Union realized that its attempts to secure an invitation to the second Bandung conference were not likely to succeed, it notified the countries concerned that it had decided to withdraw 'in order not to create divisions among the Afro-Asian states'. This was another victory for the Chinese, who deny that the Soviet Union is an Asian power and imply that its Central Asian and Far Eastern territories are ill-gotten gains of Tsarist imperialism.

But later the Soviet Union renewed its attempts to be admitted to the conference. The struggle behind the scenes reaches its climax, when the downfall of Ben Bella caused the postponement of the conference in Algiers. Despite their efforts the Chinese did not succeed in preventing the postponement, a setback which made manifest the limits of their influence among the non-aligned countries.

Afro-Asian prestige against China, when the attacks were coming from that corner.

LABEDZ: Since we have mentioned the vicissitudes of 'small countries', let us turn to a still smaller one than Yugoslavia—Albania. The Bosnians, before First World War, used to boast that 'together with the Russians' they amounted to a hundred and fifty million souls; nowadays I suppose one could say there were anything up to seven hundred million Albanians if you threw the Chinese in. How does the big Sino-Soviet issue look when seen from Tirana?

GRIFFITH: The present Albanian leaders, like all their predecessors, have been primarily concerned with one simple aim—how to keep Albania on the map at all. Since obtaining her independence in 1912 the country has only survived because her neighbours could never agree for long on any plan for carving her up. She is particularly concerned with Yugoslavia because there are half as many Albanians in that country as in Albania itself. So Albania is always looking for a protector against Yugoslavia. In Stalin's day, Russia was the bulwark against Tito. But Khrushchev would probably have been willing to abandon Albania to the tender mercies of Belgrade, so now Peking has stepped into the protector's shoes. Almost the entire motivation of communist policy in Tirana, in fact, is to be sought in this nationalist concern for protection against Yugoslavia.

LABEDZ: Considering the damage which Moscow's economic breach with Yugoslavia did to that country in Stalin's day, the exclusion of Albania from Comecon has presumably harmed that country in a somewhat similar way. It is far from clear whether the Chinese can really make up for it.

VINEY: Whatever dissatisfaction there may be in Albania because of shortages is not likely to be much greater than it was before the break with Moscow, when the supply situation was already bad enough.
    As for the possibility of a political opposition to the present Albanian leadership, this would have to be at a fairly high level to be effective and I think the people likely to express it were eliminated in the various trials up to 1961. Opposition of that kind is unlikely to recur, I should say, until the present government or party leadership had got into such difficulties that some other people at the top saw it as a chance to seize power from them. This, then, would be not so much a genuinely political opposition as a power struggle, which is always very near the

surface in a communist régime. And the cruder the régime, the nearer to the surface.

LABEDZ: In Albania the connection between the Sino-Soviet struggle outside, and the party-faction struggle inside, has been clear enough. But take Bulgaria, where we have seen so many changes in the top échelon since 1956, changes culminating in the overthrow of Vulko Chervenkov and, more recently, in the final triumph of Zhivkov over Yugov. Is there any connection here with the Sino-Soviet issue?

GRIFFITH: I think it can be demonstrated in the case of Chervenkov. Not only was he an extreme Stalinist and was presumably for that reason deposed on Khrushchev's orders in 1956, but during the following three years or so in particular he displayed pro-Chinese tendencies more frequently, perhaps, than any other east European leader out of power. This undoubtedly contributed toward his further and final disgrace.

There have been various 'revisionist' or 'national communist' elements in Bulgaria, including some, recently purged, who were not pro-Chinese. But Bulgaria and East Germany are still the most completely Soviet-controlled satellites and I think one must regard the present party leader, Zhivkov, as entirely dependent upon Soviet support.

VINEY: I would suggest that Yugov's replacement as premier by Zhivkov in 1962 was indirectly connected with the Sino-Soviet dispute. Under Yugov's premiership the Bulgarian party was more Stalinist than it has been under Zhivkov, hence Yugov was a conservative in that sense, and he was removed for that reason in addition to the internal power struggle. So there was at least an ideological link.

But at the time of the struggle leading to Yugov's removal there was also a dispute brewing up between the Soviets and Rumania. Few people in the West, indeed few in the communist camp either, knew about the existence of this dispute at the time, let alone discussed it in the press. But symptoms of disagreement about Rumanian economic policy had in fact been noticed during Khrushchev's trip to that country the previous summer. The Chinese, too, made it quite clear that they knew of these differences with Rumania and that they were prepared to play a part in them; they made it clear when Chen Yi, the Vice-Premier and Foreign Minister, turned up at an anniversary reception in the Rumanian embassy in Peking. In his speech there Chen Yi suggested that certain, unnamed, countries might be exploiting Rumania, but that China did not behave in this way toward her socialist brethren. This was not said in so many words, but the import of it was quite clear and has indeed become very much clearer since the existence of the Rumanian-Soviet dispute has been more generally accepted.

Now to return to Bulgaria, it is interesting that the only other speech of this kind was made by Chen Yi at the Bulgarian Embassy reception soon afterwards. This suggests to me that the Chinese knew something was going on between Moscow and Bulgaria too, and were hinting to the Bulgarians that they would have Chinese support in case of a showdown.

The evidence is fragmentary, but it does suggest that there may be a link between the purge of Yugov and the Sino-Soviet rift.

LABEDZ: But one cannot assume that every communist leader who is a Stalinist die-hard will automatically try to jump onto the Chinese bandwaggon. As we have seen, there has been since 1956 a general pattern of growing autonomy among the various east European communist parties, and we can now find such combinations as anti-Chinese position plus Stalinist internal rule, or vice versa. The picture is very complex. In Rumania, for example, we still have strict Stalinist controls along with a degree of economic nationalism leading inevitably to a more general reappraisal of Rumania's status within the Soviet bloc. Ulbricht, again, used to be regarded, because of his domestic Stalinism, as potentially pro-Chinese, but he has shown precious little sign of it since 1959.

In Poland, there have been retrograde tendencies in internal matters, but these have not in themselves encouraged any pro-Chinese line. If the Gomulka team have engaged in discreet manœuvres with Peking, it has not been because of any ideological affinity.

Looking at the whole of eastern Europe, then, can one say anything about the impact of the Sino-Soviet rift on the various leaders' position and policies which would be true for all?

GRIFFITH: I would revert to my opening comment and say that the only factor common to all the east European parties is that of nationalism. But for the rest—one can be Stalinist like Ulbricht and totally pro-Soviet; or anti-Stalinist like Gomulka and moderately pro-Soviet; or anti-Stalinist like Tito and more in favour of a break with China even than the Soviets are themselves.

One must, I think, distinguish three levels of differentiation when classifying the east European leaderships. The first level, perhaps the most fundamental, is the spectrum of domestic policy: revisionist —reformist—rigid-Stalinist. Here, I think, the line-up is fairly clear. Rumania, Bulgaria, East Germany and still, to some extent,

Czechoslovakia might be called extremist or Stalinist. Poland, though now less so, Yugoslavia, somewhat less so, and Hungary, now more so, can be called relatively reformist.

A second, different division is possible on the level of general international policy and, specifically, of attitudes toward the West. The four 'Stalinists' reappear here as the group more hostile to the West, but Rumania is becoming less so.

Finally there is the third criterion, perhaps the hardest to evaluate, concerning the relation of each party to the Sino-Soviet dispute itself. In present terms, the most convenient yardstick is probably the attitude of any given party to the prospect of a total and public Sino-Soviet rupture. To such a possibility the Rumanians, the Poles and probably the Hungarians are definitely opposed, and they have presumably exerted themselves with some effect to prevent it, if not so demonstratively as the Italian Party has.

VINEY: Of course, there is a difference between not wanting a rupture and not wanting a conference. The Hungarians have in fact favoured a conference, or say they do. The Rumanians are transparently clever about it, advocating—since their visit to Peking in 1964—a three-stage process for preparing a general conference and so deferring it indefinitely. And the Poles, after first opposing it altogether, declared then somewhat ambiguously that they were in favour of it.

GRIFFITH: This is all true, but I wanted to point out the contrast between these parties and the Czechs, Bulgarians and East Germans who are totally pro-Soviet and favour a conference when Moscow favours it, oppose it when Moscow opposes; and still more with the Yugoslavs and Albanians, who each want a total break at any cost —whether the principals in the dispute want it or not! The object: for the Yugoslavs, to preserve their special position with the Soviets; for the Albanians, to preserve theirs with Mao.

LABEDZ: I am not sure one can so simply equate the Albanian and Yugoslav attitudes toward a final rupture. Albania is no doubt mortally afraid of any *rapprochement* between the Russians and the Chinese since this would mean the disappearance of the 'protector' which their foreign policy toward Yugoslavia so absolutely requires. The Yugoslavs also dread any genuine Sino-Soviet reconciliation, since this would deprive them of the double advantage they now enjoy, viz. close relations with the Soviet Union combined with freedom of manœuvre in foreign policy arising from the Sino-Soviet quarrel. But it does not follow that they want a public break, and there were some articles in the Yugoslav press recently opposing a world communist conference in the near future. The question of this conference has, of course, become a touchstone of total versus less-than-total commitment to the Soviet line. Togliatti's visit to Belgrade was relevant to this. For the Italian Party, though strongly anti-Chinese in ideology, at the same time opposes the holding of a conference that would formalize the break. The joint communiqué issued by the two parties confirmed that the Yugoslavs take into account various considerations praised by the Italians.

VINEY: I should like to take up this point about the Italian Communist Party, for I think we are witnessing the beginning of a period in which these west European parties are going to try to stake out for themselves positions of some independence. I believe we should accept the possibility that eastern Europe is not going to be quite as important in the international communist movement as it has been, once parties like those of France and Italy assume larger roles. As evidence for the Italian Party's role, we have the Party's rejection of an international communist conference to condemn China, even though this proposal originated in Moscow; and the Italian communists' attempts to organize a conference to be attended by the parties of western Europe.

The Italian Party's statement of 24 October 1963, expressing reservations about a general conference, also went into considerable detail on the ideological and political position of communism. In a remarkable passage it suggested that 'Stalinist deformations' in both the Soviet Union and east Europe had put, and were still putting, weapons into the hands of the enemies of communism. That was really a way of saying, as the Italian communists so often have said, that unless the Soviet and east European parties went much further along the path of liberalization, they would hinder any political progress by western communists.

LABEDZ: Could a separate evolution of west European communism lead to the east European parties moving closer to the western ones, making the pattern of relations between the world's communist parties still more complex?

VINEY: I should say this is already happening. Griffith pointed out that the Rumanians and, on and off, the Poles are on the same side as the Italians on the question of an international communist conference. Of course, their motives don't tally and the three parties display a great contrast in complexion. But the interesting and perhaps welcome thing is the development of such little communist ententes in these polycentric days. The Italian Party is a useful ally for Dej because, though not in power, it is big and it might be. It might be, that is, if it persuaded enough Italian voters that they would be happier under a communist régime. Insofar as the Rumanian régime makes rude gestures, or highly independent ones, in Moscow's direction, that is good propaganda for Italian communists. Unfortunately, though, the Rumanian régime is also a relatively Stalinist one. How much better for Marxist orators in Turin or Bologna if the slow process of liberalization in east Europe were visibly to speed up! What looks like relative freedom in Bucharest still looks like relative slavery to spoilt westerners. So far as the voting public in Italy can see, the changes in eastern Europe have not been great enough to earn more votes for the Italian Communist Party or to make a communist régime seem desirable in Italy.

If such changes are to have any effect at all in western Europe, they must be far more radical than they have been to date.

LABEDZ: Returning to opinion in east Europe, I do not think there is any likelihood of *that* public being over-impressed by the speed of de-Stalinization either. But it might perhaps be influenced by something else that we have not yet touched upon, namely the consequences of the attempt to unify east Europe economically through Comecon. What are these consequences likely to be, particularly in the new Sino-Soviet context?

GRIFFITH: Part of Khrushchev's response to the Chinese defiance has been a serious attempt—the most serious Soviet attempt yet—to bring about a genuine, multilateral, economic integration of eastern Europe. The project has been favoured by east Europeans like Gomulka and Kádár, who feel they can gain by it. It has been strongly, and successfully, opposed by the Rumanian leader Gheorghiu Dej, who correctly surmises that at present the total multilateral economic integration of eastern Europe would prevent the across-the-board industrialization of his own country.

But though the Khrushchev project is a response to China in one way, it is perhaps even more a response to the enormous economic growth of western Europe. It is a reaction, then, to the two most significant shifts in the balance of power over the past five years. Add to these the strategic thermo-nuclear lead of the United States, and Khrushchev's own grain shortage and general economic crisis at home, and you have a pattern of Soviet failure of which, it seems to me, much of the failure in eastern Europe is simply a reflection. A prime example of this failure is the country we have scarcely mentioned yet—the satellite that orbits most timorously and closely to the Soviet field of gravity—East Germany. Here the contrast between eastern economic failure and western success is at its ironic sharpest, and so is the failure to achieve Khrushchev's strategic and political No. 1 priority aim of a few years back—neutralization of Berlin and consolidation of the division of Germany; and so, finally, is the failure to achieve a tolerable degree of popularity and real strength for Ulbricht's régime. The Berlin Wall is an ominously solid and durable symbol of all these failures.

VINEY: On the general issue of Comecon I think it needs to be said that that attempt at economic integration has had a more disruptive effect politically on eastern Europe than any other issue of recent years. The attempt at integration of economies has, most notably in the case of Rumania, simply provided the stimulus for a show of autonomy; the mere discussion of economic integration has provided the framework for a struggle by each country to carve out as much as it can for itself—economically and hence politically too. One result is freer trading policies. Witness the acceptance of Federal German trading missions by Poland, Hungary, Rumania, Bulgaria—perhaps by Czechoslovakia soon.

LABEDZ: Taking the long view, it could or should have been expected that if communism was going to win its victories in the undeveloped countries then the problem of economic nationalism would automatically exacerbate that of nationalism in general. Differences were bound to arise about industrialization and the question of who is going to contribute how much to investment, what sort and where. The inability or unwillingness of the Russians to help more with China's industrialization was a prime bone of contention between them, and economic aid from Russia, as a relatively developed country, is a question affecting both her relations with the poorer communist régimes and theirs with each other. This question simply was not within the communist ideological purview before the assumption of power by a plurality of communist régimes. And now eastern Europe is facing this issue with a vengeance, precisely at a time when western Europe seems to be finding political solutions which do not provoke economic nationalism—the Common Market with its expectation of reaching a stage of complete customs union in a few years. In the East, economic integration problems loom very large and may be hard to solve within the framework of communist state relations, of which the Sino-Soviet conflict sets such a daunting example. Coordination of economic plans seems impossible, in fact, without either a single political authority, or else a common market type of institution; and neither is likely to emerge in eastern Europe at present. Is it possible to forecast what *will* emerge?

GRIFFITH: Somebody said that 'prophecy is the most gratuitous form of error', but I think we can well content ourselves for the moment with considering what *is* emerging already. And that is, on the one hand, a general differentiation of communism in eastern Europe, as the various countries secure not withdrawal of Soviet control, but a transmutation of Soviet control, in quantity and quality, that gives these countries greater autonomy; secondly, an accentuation of nationalism; and finally the desire and the new ability of the various eastern European régimes to give rein to their nationalism, sometimes so long and reluctantly repressed, in this expanding and loosening framework of autonomy. This is the sort of situation that produces confusion more often than tidy trends, and if we refrain from forecasting we can do so with a good conscience!

4
The Parties
around China

SPEAKERS

Donald S. Zagoria

Patrick J. Honey

Leopold Labedz

4. The Parties around China

LABEDZ: Coming to the impact of the Sino-Soviet split on Asia, I would suggest that we concentrate on the relationship between the Chinese Communist Party and the communist parties on the periphery of China, such as the Korean, Indonesian, North-Vietnamese and Indian parties.

Geography, traditional ties, and, where they exist, bonds of a common civilization—these are the three factors which seem to me to be of paramount importance. What significance would you attribute to the power-nexus which exists between a large country such as China and her smaller or, at any rate, less powerful neighbours; and, secondly, how does the fact that some of these countries are ruled by communist parties determine their attitude to China and the Soviet Union?

HONEY: In all the countries we are discussing tonight the dominating factors of the situation are geographic and economic. Most of the countries, particularly those ruled by communist governments, rely for foreign aid, especially foreign technical help, mainly on the Soviet Union. They are all backward countries industrially and in order to build up their industrial base and to bring them into the twentieth century they have to draw on Soviet resources and techniques. And since many of them have had vassal relations with China in the past and since all of them are acutely aware of the growing strength, particularly the numerical strength, of the Chinese army, they have to balance their needs for Russian economic and technical aid against the possible reaction of China if they go over too far on to the Russian side of the dispute.

Here you have a conflict between geographical interests and internal economic interests. For most of the Asian countries, or for very many of them, this is the principal difficulty which is posed by the Sino-Soviet dispute.

LABEDZ: Do you think that this dilemma is in fact general? What about countries such as Japan for instance, or Indonesia, where the communist parties are not in power? Does the conflict affect all countries on the periphery of China?

ZAGORIA: I would be inclined to put more stress on the relationship of some of these countries with the United States. One of the basic reasons why the Chinese have been unhappy with Soviet policy for so many years is that from the Chinese viewpoint Soviet policy means coming to something of an understanding with the United States and therefore an indefinite preservation of the *status quo* in Asia; at least it makes it less likely that American political and military power will be removed from the western Pacific, a factor inhibiting Chinese goals in Asia.

I think the same problem is posed for the North Koreans and the North Vietnamese, who both realise that only a very tough, militant, anti-American line is likely to get the Americans out of the southern halves of their countries. The war in the south was largely the reason why the North Vietnamese have been gradually pushed into Chinese arms, just as it was the problem of South Korea which pushed the North Koreans at an earlier point closer to China.

The same thing is true even in a country like Japan, where one of the reasons why the Japanese Communist Party is leaning closer to China is that the leading faction in the Japanese Party believes that you need a two-stage revolution in Japan; at the first stage you remove American political and military influence rather than try to push a socialist revolution all at once.

LABEDZ: I wonder if the question of the strategic influence of America in the western Pacific is as decisive as you make out. Surely it does not hold good in respect of India, for instance. The general geopolitical situation of that country is rather different from that of Indonesia, or Japan, or Vietnam. Would not the Sino-Soviet split affect all these peripheral parties even if there was no American presence in South East Asia? Going by the book, the countries where the communist party is in power are supposed to be on good terms with each other. Their relations are supposed to be devoid of antagonisms, of divergences of interest, of all traditional enmities. I rather suspect that such a supposition is entirely utopian. History shows that a communist party in power does not at all mean the extinction of nationalism. The fact that the communists have nowhere been successful unless they could ride the wave of nationalism speaks for itself and carries with it a question mark for the future: the problem of the relations between communist states as distinct from communist parties. The question of the American presence or lack of it in a particular area is thus incidental, to my mind, to the basic problem of relations between communist states.

HONEY: Japan and Indonesia, being island states, are obviously less worried about the vicinity of the Chinese army than are the mainland countries; and, although one may think of India as being on the outer periphery, the Chinese attack on India made the Indians think once again. However much they might persuade themselves that they are remote from Chinese influence, events have shown that they are not.

In the case of Japan the problems there are perhaps untypical of the rest of Asia, simply because Japan has now made herself into a modern mid-twentieth-century industrial power. She has a very different set of problems to deal with than, for example, the communists in Indonesia.

Equally, when you talk about the possible spread of communism you cannot ignore the historical fact that communism usually does not contrive to establish itself in a country without outside help. The Chinese are very much aware of this; that is why they are concentrating their attention perhaps more on countries like North Vietnam, Laos, Burma and indeed India. All of these countries are a springboard to something else. North Korea, on the other hand, only leads to South Korea and I think it attracts far less attention from the Chinese for that reason.

LABEDZ: Let us take two countries which are contiguous to the two protagonists: Korea and Mongolia. We know that when the quarrel between the Chinese and the Russian communists was heating up these two countries reacted quite differently. Mongolia has now become firmly pro-Russian and joined Comecon. The North Korean leaders first tried to sit on the fence and then came down gradually on the Chinese side.

Why did these two countries react in such different ways and why have they chosen exactly the opposite position *vis-à-vis* the Sino-Soviet conflict?

ZAGORIA: I would venture to say that one important difference is that the Russians have always had a great deal more sheer physical control in Mongolia than in Korea.

LABEDZ: But there was trouble in the country going back many years before the conflict; the Mongolian people were by no means so friendly towards the Russians. There had been purges inside the Mongolian Party* and there was, of course, the competition between China

* The existence of a nationalist opposition within the leadership of the Mongolian Communist Party was revealed by the Mongolian Premier, Yumzhagin Tsedanbal, in his December 1964 speech at the plenary meeting of the Central Committee of the Party. He disclosed that the leader of the 'anti-Party group', Timur Ochir, was excluded from the Mongolian politbureau in 1962, and a member of the Central Committee, Tsende, was expelled from it in 1963. Three other members, Lokhouz, Niamtz, and Surmajap, suffered the same fate after Tsedanbal's speech. He accused them of causing 'grave damage to the cause of the Party'.

and Russia. But until the emergence of China as a communist country, the problem looked very different, because China was politically prostrate.

As we know, the Russians eventually came out on top. But was this because they had physical control of the country, or was it because they had more to offer? Or were there other reasons?

HONEY: Mongolia is in the happy position of being a buffer state, which makes it very tempting for both sides to try and woo her. When a communist country is in as happy a position as this, then the amount of aid either side can give her will be of paramount importance. After all, if you are poised between Russia and China and both sides are courting you and offering you their favours, then you are in a position simply to sit back and raise your price. Any sensible country would have opted for the Russians, because the Soviet Union can give Mongolia so much more than China. If you look at Mongolia today you will see that this policy has paid off very handsomely.

Korea on the other hand is perhaps at the very opposite end of the scale. Geographically she is adjacent to China, but Kim Ir Sung, the party leader, has always been looking primarily towards Moscow. One must, therefore, ask onself why he has changed his allegiance from Moscow to Peking and I am not convinced that the geographical factor will entirely account for this. I think the geographical factor is very important, but I also suspect that at some time, when he displeased the Russians, they probably engaged in some manœuvre to replace him. If this did in fact happen—I have no positive proof of it—then he would naturally turn towards the Chinese.

The position of Korea is directly affected by two contradictory elements. She is adjacent to China and therefore has to avoid giving offence to China. She is, on the other hand, almost entirely dependent upon the Soviet Union for technological aid. She has been quite clearly trying to balance these two factors, and although she has come down very strongly indeed on the side of the Chinese, she has not come completely off the fence.

LABEDZ: Some of the parties on the periphery of China which have taken a pro-Chinese stand nevertheless hesitate to take this last step and make their position unambiguous. The Chinese came out into the open already on 14 June 1963, calling the Russians by name, not only condemning them but actually abusing them. The Koreans confine themselves to attacking modern revisionists, which is, of course, the term designed specially for the Soviet leadership. But it is not calling a spade a spade.

64

ZAGORIA: One of the interesting questions one might ask in this connection is why the Koreans were, as I think they were, the earliest Chinese ally. North Korean support for the Chinese in the Sino-Soviet dispute goes back at least to 1960. They certainly supported the Chinese at the Moscow Conference in 1960 and they were in the field alongside the Chinese before the Albanians. This was at a time when the North Vietnamese and all the other parties in Asia were still scrabbling.

Again I would advance a strategic reason. The most important problem facing the North Korean leadership was, and is, how to re-unify Korea. The issue between Russia and China in 1960 must have appeared to them primarily as a question of whether there was going to be a bloc-wide policy of militant struggle designed to remove the Americans from South Korea and the rest of the western Pacific. The North Korean leaders probably thought, and still think, that the chances of reunification are better served by Peking, and they may well be right.

LABEDZ: What does the situation look like in a country such as Japan which is neither adjacent to China nor ruled by a communist party?

HONEY: Japan is a special case and I would certainly go along with Zagoria's argument that the revolution is seen by the Japanese communists as being a two-stage affair: get rid of the Americans first, then work for an understanding with China. China offers an enormous market for Japanese products and she is right on Japan's doorstep which must also sway the Japanese to a *rapprochement* with the Chinese.

LABEDZ: There is a curious coincidence of attitudes between the Japanese Communist Party and certain representatives of Japanese big business: there have been businessmen going to China trying to explore the market there. The bait of a large and hungry receptacle in China is constantly dangled before the eyes of these people. On the other hand, one must remember that the tough line which the Japanese communists have now adopted will not improve their electoral prospects. They have abandoned the previous image of the Party, the 'lovable' party, as they liked to call it, and they know that it would be foolish of them to think of a revolutionary seizure of power. Also, the Party's disapproval of the test-ban treaty adds to its handicaps because, as we know, Japanese public opinion is extremely sensitive on this subject. What then explains the position taken by the Japanese leaders, who were not compelled to make the kind of choice which the North

Vietnamese and the North Koreans had to make? They could have played a variant of communist neutralism in the Sino-Soviet dispute. But although they have expressed their attitude in the most obscure language, they have nevertheless moved very close to identifying themselves with the Chinese.*

ZAGORIA: I think there are several reasons for all this. One is the communists' relationship with the socialist party in Japan† which is, after all, the most politically significant Marxist party there; it got almost thirty per cent of the vote in the last elections and is the principal opposition party to the Liberal Democrats. The problem for the Japanese communists, if they were to pursue the softer Khrushchevian line of aligning themselves in a national front with the other left-wing parties, would be their fear of submersion both in organization and ideologically. Their problem is exactly the reverse of that of the Italian Communist Party which tends to align itself with the socialists, inasmuch as in Italy the communists can hold their own in such an alliance, whereas in Japan the communists are weak and might easily lose their identity as a separate force.

Also there are close personal ties between some of the Japanese communist leaders and the Chinese. Sanzo Nosaka, for example, looks back rather wistfully in some of his writings to his days in Yenan, but he does not look back so wistfully to his days in Moscow. Several of

* In May 1964 they expelled two of their nine representatives in the Diet because both voted for the ratification of the test-ban treaty, and in June 1964 eight more members of the Party were rusticated. Some of these then proceeded to publish a new pro-Soviet weekly, *The Voices of Japan*, which was promptly hailed by *Pravda* as a paper that will 'rally all comrades who were unjustly expelled' and 'uphold the correct line'. The removal of Yoshio Shiga and Ichizo Suzuki virtually ended the process of purging the Party from its pro-Soviet elements which began in 1961 with the expulsion of Shojiro Kasuga's group.

† The Russians are now openly courting, or are pushed into courting, the socialists, and this has already got them into very strange situations. In August 1964, rival anti-nuclear conferences were held by the Japanese communists and the Japanese socialists. The Russians had instructed their delegation to attend both, but at the communist meeting, which was controlled by pro-Chinese delegates, the Russians and their sympathizers were shouted down and excluded from key committees.

They had no choice but to walk out in protest. The next thing they did was to throw their weight behind the rival meeting. The piquancy of the situation is not only that in Japan Moscow lost a foothold in the Communist Party, but that the Russians' attempt to further cooperation with the socialists (and thus possibly ally themselves with a non-communist party) may be frustrated because the left wing of the Socialist Party is pro-Chinese, and the socialist leaders are afraid that too close an involvement with either side may undermine the unity of the party.

66

the high-ranking leaders in the Japanese Party fled to China right at the beginning of the Korean war when the Party went underground and stayed there for a number of years. There were, and there probably still are, schools in mainland China training Japanese party leaders for an eventual revolution in Japan.

Moreover there is an important cultural factor both in Japan and in Korea. Not only members of the Communist Party, but the Japanese and Koreans generally feel themselves to be part of a common civilisation; they all use Chinese characters. In Japan this is a somewhat ambiguous feeling because the Japanese are, at the same time, very proud of the fact that it was they who modernized first and not the Chinese. All the same, there is a great respect, if not awe, for Chinese civilization in Japan, and it would be very surprising if an element which cuts across the whole culture did not affect the Communist Party.

LABEDZ: If, as you suggest, the tough line taken by the Japanese party was motivated by the fear that they might be submerged in the Socialist Party or a front organisation, how do you square this with communist policy in Indonesia, where the communists take part in the 'guided democracy' of Soekarno?

Are the Indonesian comrades not in danger of forfeiting their identity?

HONEY: I think you have a number of factors in Indonesia which are peculiar to that country. For example, you have the curious governmental structure with Soekarno at the top of what can almost be described as a triangle: the Indonesian Communist Party forming one of the arms of the triangle and the Indonesian army forming the other. These two are rivals and Soekarno can, and does, play one off against the other.

Secondly you have in Indonesia the problem of an indigenous Chinese community which has in the past led the Indonesian Party into difficulties. The party would therefore have every reason to watch them and not move too close to the Chinese.

Thirdly, Indonesia is an island state and therefore the influence of China upon her is less direct than on the mainland states. I think you have to take all these factors into account. The line adopted by the Indonesian Party is probably dictated as much by local factors as by ideological considerations.

LABEDZ: Zagoria has just returned from Indonesia and has seen several leaders of the Indonesian Communist Party including M. H. Lukman, its deputy leader. Can you tell us from your personal experience how the Indonesian Party sees its own position towards the Sino-Soviet split?

ZAGORIA: Their position has been, and continues to be, that they are not passively sitting by, that they are active participants in this dispute between the Russians and the Chinese. They insist that they are taking an independent line. At the same time in most of the important cases they have been closer to the Chinese, the test ban being one important example on which they have taken essentially the Chinese position.*

The question as to why the Indonesian Party takes this pro-Chinese position is one that has been puzzling me. The Indonesian party is pursuing what can only be called (and has been called by some Indian communists with whom I talked) an opportunist strategy of the first order. They are cooperating with a 'bourgeois nationalist', Soekarno. Soekarno addresses their party congresses. The leaders in the Indonesian Communist Party talk to the Defence College, they address the Staff Academy at the Foreign Affairs Ministry, and when I asked Lukman what he talks to the army officers about, he said, 'I talk to them about Marxism and Leninism'. The army officers sit in on their party congresses and take notes. The party pledged itself not to encourage strikes in the trade unions it dominates. It is pursuing a strategy that one would think is the complete antithesis of the line that the Chinese have been recommending to all Asian parties and specifically warning against, namely sacrificing one's organizational integrity and militancy to the 'bourgeois nationalists'. At the same time that they are taking this ultra-opportunist line they are siding with China. Clearly, this cannot be explained on ideological or strategic grounds; it seems to me that here one has to look for such things as nationalism and even racialism. As one Indonesian fellow-traveller put it to me, they just felt closer to China than to Russia which is ethnically and culturally very distant. Also, when Indonesians talk about anti-imperialism—they talk a great deal about it, not only the Indonesian communists but Soekarno as well—to them it means at the moment the struggle against Malaysia and the communists are very much a part of this struggle because this is one of the ways they see of increasing their own power position in Indonesia. They have more or less indicated that the Russians, by pursuing a softer line internationally, were bound to let up on this struggle against imperialism in South East Asia and that this would result in a stabilisation of the *status quo*.

* In July 1964 the Indonesian Party passed a resolution opposing Soviet proposals for a world meeting of communist parties 'without full preparations'. This was obviously Peking's unofficial reply to Moscow's call for an early conference.

LABEDZ: In fact, when one looks more closely at any of these situations one sees how *sui generis* each one of them is. The element of nationalism in the Indonesian Communist Party has been very pronounced and it was very conspicuous in Aidit's speech in February, 1963, before the Indonesian Party's plenum. In Peking, in September 1963, Aidit completely identified his position on a number of issues with the Chinese Party, he stressed the need for militancy and he went so far as to support the activity of various small pro-Chinese groups trying to split the established communist parties in underdeveloped countries and in the West. Nevertheless he again strongly emphasized the specific characteristics of the Indonesian situation and he spoke highly of the *Nasakom* slogan which includes not only nationalism but religion too. So the response in each case seems to be dictated largely by local considerations.

Moving from Indonesia to North Vietnam: what are the specific elements which determine the present line of the Ho Chi Minh régime *vis-à-vis* the Sino-Soviet split? We know that Ho Chi Minh was trying very hard to avoid committing himself, that he was making trips to Moscow *and* China. Also there is a good deal of traditional feeling against the Chinese in what used to be called Indo-China. Nevertheless the North-Vietnamese régime is pro-Chinese in the Sino-Soviet dispute in much the same way as Indonesia and North Korea. How is one to explain this?

HONEY: Ho Chi Minh's position is perhaps the most difficult of all the Asian communist leaders insofar as he is controlling a state which is not viable. He finds himself right on the borders of China and he has a 'national liberation war' going in South Vietnam.

Let me first say that North Vietnam is largely mountainous, it is over-populated in relation to its agricultural area, consequently it suffers from a recurring shortage of food. This was proved during French times; the rice surplus from South Vietnam was always bought up by the French to balance the rice deficit in North Vietnam so that right from the word 'go' Ho Chi Minh has been struggling against this inherent difficulty of his state.

In the very early days he carried through a Chinese-type agrarian reform which cut down agricultural production even further and increased his difficulties.

Ho Chi Minh then appears to have decided that the answer to his problems in North Vietnam was, first to create very rapidly an industrial base, set up factories, start manufacturing goods, export these goods and with the foreign currency thus earned buy food and raise his internal living standards. He is dependent almost entirely for his technological aid upon the Soviet Union and upon eastern Europe. On the other hand, his geographical position and the historical factor that Vietnam, particularly North Vietnam, was in the past under Chinese suzerainty, makes his position very vulnerable *vis-à-vis* the neighbouring Chinese. Therefore his problem was to get the maximum technological aid from Russia and east Europe, while, at the same time, avoiding any offence to China.

He has done this with commendable skill for a number of years. Yet his aid from Russia and eastern Europe has not been nearly as great as he imagined it would be, and for that reason his industrialization programme has moved very slowly. His industrial capacity at the moment is small. He has avoided giving offence to the Chinese, staying on the fence more skilfully than any other Asian Communist leader. What finally brought him down from the fence was the test-ban treaty. He was told from Moscow that he had got to sign it. He was told from Peking that he had got to refuse to sign it. There simply was no room for manœuvre. He had to make up his mind what he was going to do because if he did nothing at all, this would be a refusal to sign and therefore it would put him in the Chinese camp. I have no doubt at all that there were rows within the Politburo of the party before the decision was made, because he has a strong pro-Chinese and a strong pro-Soviet faction in his party, and finally it was decided that they would refuse to sign because the danger of the proximity of the Chinese was overwhelming.*

Secondly, when he signed the Geneva agreements in 1954, which split the country into two, Ho Chi Minh fully expected South Vietnam to collapse under the weight of her own internal dissensions and fall like a ripe plum into his lap. In fact this did not happen. The United States gave very generous aid to South Vietnam and Ngo Dinh Diem took unexpectedly vigorous action against the opposing political factions in South Vietnam; 1956 saw a South Vietnam with a strong government, and, thanks to United States aid, economic progress was being made, whereas in North Vietnam, contrary to what had been

* Since that time there is evidence of a fairly rapid decline in Russian technological aid which has resulted in increasing economic hardship. Indeed, so precarious has the economy become that a sizeable faction of the North Vietnamese Party has begun to struggle for a reversal of the present pro-Chinese line and a return to closer links with the Soviet Union. Although members of this faction have not been able to publish any criticism of the present line, they have been very active, causing worry to the majority faction, which is pro-Chinese. During the first half of 1964 the North Vietnamese press published many articles attacking the pro-Soviet faction. Despite these attacks, the pro-Soviet Vietnamese have not abandoned their struggle; the factional struggle has become more intense since the bombing of North Vietnam began.

expected, and largely owing to the Chinese-type agrarian reforms, there was a falling standard of life and an increasing shortage of food.

After some time Ho Chi Minh decided that the only answer to his food shortage was to get his hands on the rice bowl of South Vietnam, and one saw about mid-1959 a resurgence of guerrilla warfare. This was met by American military aid to South Vietnam and when the Sino-Soviet dispute started, which was not so very long after the resurgence of fighting, the war was not terribly welcome in Moscow. Peking, on the other hand, could afford to give all the encouragement Ho Chi Minh wanted. He was in an extremely difficult position which I do not think has improved to this day.

LABEDZ: As we have seen in the case of North Korea, local nationalism intermingles with the struggle between the pro-Chinese and pro-Soviet factions in the party and the same is true of North Vietnam. But there is one difference. While the problem of succession at the top in North Korea is not on the agenda, the succession of Ho Chi Minh, who is an elderly man, probably looms large in the minds of the communist leaders of North Vietnam. I wonder if this problem of succession will in any way affect the political leanings of the North Vietnamese Party?

ZAGORIA: I do not think this is a question of personalities, either in North Vietnam, China or anywhere else. I would be very surprised if the death of Ho Chi Minh would lead to a resurgence of pro-Moscow people in the north, and I think the reasons why Ho Chi Minh has moved closer to China have been well outlined by Honey. The thing that stands out in my mind is the food problem, the need to reunify North Vietnam with southern rice.

I heard a rather interesting story from a member of the International Commission in South Vietnam. According to him the problem, as the North Vietnamese saw it, was that right after the Laotian settlement in 1962, the North Vietnamese felt 'If the Americans are going to give us a neutral Laos, maybe with a little prodding they will be prepared to give us a neutral South Vietnam.' This, from their point of view, was not an unrealistic assumption because there were many people in the United States who did not understand why Laos and South Vietnam were being divorced and thought they should be regarded as parts of one issue. The North Vietnamese thus could easily have arrived at a conclusion that they were part of a whole in American thinking and that the Americans would give them a neutral South Vietnam, having agreed to a neutral Laos.

It did not turn out that way, so they thought that to bag the South would require a little extra prodding and they intensified the guerrilla war. By the fall of 1961 South Vietnam was on the verge of collapse; and it was at this time that the Taylor mission first came and introduced a large American military assistance programme. What was happening, in short, was that the situation in the south looked very good from the northern point of view because it was a fragile political structure which the communists thought they could easily push over. Within a year or so Ho Chi Minh's people were enjoying great success. By 1962–1963 to pull out of this situation was unthinkable, and to stay in required Chinese support.

LABEDZ: So we have here a curious paradox whereby anti-Chinese nationalism produces, for a variety of reasons, support for the Chinese line. In the case of India, however, the pro-Chinese and nationalist factions are clearly divided. Perhaps in no other country is the struggle between the pro-Chinese and pro-Soviet factions so sharp and clear as it is in India. After the 1962 fighting in Ladakh the pro-Chinese faction in the Communist Party, which was pretty strong, although it formed a minority in the central committee, was pushed out of the leadership. This was partly due to Nehru's firm action and partly to the work of the pro-Soviet wing, headed by Dange, who exploited it with considerable skill. Now almost two years have passed and we have seen ups and downs in the fortunes of the Indian party factions. All these twists and turns were intimately connected with the Indian party's very real predicament of having to face both the Sino-Soviet split and the conflict between China and India.

HONEY: India is a problem all on its own. In addition to the national problems of the Communist Party in India, one has a variety of local problems. Conditions in the various states which made up India are so very different that it is hardly surprising that the Indian Communist Party is divided. It is split on all kinds of regional issues, and one had this division already before the Chinese attack came in on India.

This invasion of Indian territory had a very great emotional effect upon all Indians including a large number of the Indian communists. For the pro-Moscow wing of the Indian Communist Party it must have been a godsend; from the point of view of the pro-Chinese, of course, nothing worse could have happened. But nothing seems to be terribly logical in India; after the Chinese attack one might have expected that the Bengali branch of the party, which was nearest to the scene of invasion, would go over to the pro-Soviet wing, but in fact the Bengalis have been the leaders of the pro-Chinese faction.

LABEDZ: Although some of the pro-Chinese leaders are still in prison (January 1964), the pro-Chinese faction has been trying to recover its position, and several important party leaders are now straddling the fence.* I have in mind such people as Namboodiripad, the ex-Chief Minister of Kerala. Now that the first emotional response to the Chinese attack on Indian territory has petered out, how do you see the future of the pro-Chinese wing in the Indian party?

ZAGORIA: The impression I got from talking with some of the Indian communists and people in India was that over the years the Indian Communist Party has been moving more and more towards the right. The estimate I heard of left wing or pro-Chinese strength in the Indian Party was something like thirty per cent. I do not think the pro-Peking faction can therefore take over the Party. Moreover some of the people who make up the thirty per cent were having second thoughts about the Chinese position while they were in gaol, and are now pursuing a middle-of-the-road, if still somewhat pro-Chinese, line.† The interesting point is that the left wing seems to be quite strong in those three areas where the Communist Party has something of a mass base, namely Kerala, Andhra and West Bengal. I do not know how one would explain this, but in effect this means that the only organizational basis for the right wing is in the trade unions which it controls, while the left wing seems to have a much more solid base in the peasant movement, particularly in Kerala, where the two factions have put up separate candidates at the local elections.

LABEDZ: If I may make a brief summary here, in Stalin's time we

* But later, in exactly the same way as the 'uncommitted' communist parties in Asia abandoned their 'neutralism' when the Sino-Soviet dispute became more intensive, the 'centrists' in the Indian party found their position on the fence uncomfortable, and as a result they have joined the 'leftists', with whom they differ on many issues. In April 1964, thirty-two left-wing rebels, including the 'centrists', E.M.S. Namboodiripad and Jyoti Basu, were suspended from the National Council for opposing the pro-Soviet leadership of Chairman Dange. In June 1964 the conflict between the pro-Soviet and pro-Chinese factions became so heated that, in the state of Andhra, fighting broke out between them and 1,500 houses were burned down in the process. In November the 'leftists' held a Party Congress (a month before the Congress of the 'rightist' CPI), proclaiming a rival communist party, which already existed in all but name. The 'leftists' have their own organization and several journals in vernacular languages; they also publish pamphlets in English. But 800 of them, including most of their leaders, were arrested by the Indian government and kept in preventive detention. Namboodiripad and Jyoti Basu, however, were left free.

† In 1964 it was the 'leftists' who were in the ascendant, and the 'rightists' who were on the defensive. The personal position of Dange has been undermined by the publication of his highly damaging letters from prison, which he described as 'forgery', while failing to bring the case to court.

3*   73

were used to looking at the position of these parties in terms of what was, after all, a myth of monolithic communism; now, when we look at each party, it is the differences that strike us. It is the specific elements in each situation which draw our attention because, as we have seen, the stance taken by each party is predominantly determined by local factors. Without the knowledge of these one cannot really understand why the leaders of these Asian parties opt for one particular line of policy rather than another.

Nevertheless, there are certain common elements, and the fact that, despite great local differences, so many of these parties have taken a more or less openly pro-Chinese line seems to call for additional explanation.

If one were to put it in a few words, what would be the most important factors to stress?

HONEY: The thing that strikes me most is the paradoxical fact that China, which has been for so long the philosophical defender of universalism, should have been the one country which has split universalism and broken up the monolith. It has split it up into its various factions, and perhaps the most important lesson to be learnt from this is that whenever one talks of universalism, after one's experience of what has happened in the Sino-Soviet dispute, one is very quickly brought down to earth by the facts of the individual cases which we have been discussing. In the light of this it is clear that whether you are communist, conservative, or socialist or whatever you are, your policy in your own particular country and your own particular country's policy in international affairs, are always going to be dictated primarily by national reasons within your own country rather than any doctrine.

ZAGORIA: I think it has taken the Sino-Soviet dispute to demonstrate that there is a common glue binding together many of the Asian revolutionaries, nationalists and communists alike. M. N. Roy once said that communism in Asia is nationalism painted red. I think this is quite true. I would go further: it seems to me that nationalism in Asia is the kind of anti-imperialist, anti-European, anti-white nationalism which is now increasingly coming to the fore and which I think is a very important element in explaining why, in quite different situations, these Asian communist parties are forming a near-coalition with the Chinese.

LABEDZ: When M. N. Roy said that communism in Asia is nationalism painted red, he did not, of course, envisage that one day it may turn out to be nationalism painted yellow.

74

5

The Parties in the Underdeveloped Countries

SPEAKERS

David L. Morison

William Adie

Leopold Labedz

5. The Parties in the Underdeveloped Countries

LABEDZ: The history of communist attitudes toward the colonial countries began to take shape at the 1921 Baku Conference and in the resolution of the Comintern's second congress. For a movement which had originally expected that the proletarian revolution would start in the industrially advanced countries, it was always something of a problem that revolutionary attitudes should, in fact, have become most apparent in backward countries instead.

During the lifetime of Stalin, with his doctrine of the two camps, there was no room for a 'third world'; he was most hostile toward any idea that the underdeveloped countries should constitute a non-aligned grouping. After Stalin's death, however, the Soviet government changed their policy and started wooing the ex-colonial countries which had gained their independence after the Second World War. But this raised a new problem for communists: how to combine support for the nationalist governments in those countries, most of which were professing faith in non-alignment and neutralism, with the promotion of revolution in the self-same regions. And the problem has become all the more acute since the Chinese challenged Soviet policy and accused the Russians of betraying the national liberation movements.

MORISON: Differences between the Soviet and Chinese attitudes to the 'national liberation movement'—which in practice simply means 'nationalism'—were apparent before the split, and do not seem to have unduly worried the Russians then. In 1959, for example, the Soviet journal *International Affairs* carried a discussion between Russian and Chinese contributors in which you could clearly sense the contrast—the Chinese calling for more support for armed liberation movements while the Russians emphasized that revolutions are not necessarily armed at all.

To jump from that time right up to the present, an interesting new note struck by the Russians is that the Soviet system offers the new countries 'intellectual attraction'. They need 'social progress', Khrushchev has stressed, and they cannot attain it only on revolutionary battlefields. These ideas are aimed at the intelligentsia of the new countries, to which category most of the leaders of these countries belong.

Another point at issue between Russians and Chinese is the racial one. The Russians deplore any overt appeal to racial sentiments and accuse the Chinese of saying that the coloured peoples must stick together—a category which might or might not include the Chinese but could certainly not be stretched to embrace the Russians.

A more fundamental Soviet objection to the Chinese line is that it makes, or so the Russians complain, the national liberation movement more important than the communist movement itself as the instrument for defeating 'imperialism'. At one time, accordingly, the Russians started to down-grade the national liberation movement but then, finding that this put them in a difficult position *vis-à-vis* Asian and particularly African nationalists, had to up-grade it again.

Finally, the Russians seem to be worried that the Chinese line may make a greater appeal to the emotions of the third world. In one of their open letters, in fact, the Soviet Communist Party found it necessary to complain of people who 'play on the emotions of the masses' —and things have surely come to a pretty pass if communists cannot be permitted to play on the feelings of the common people! More recently, again, the Russians have spoken of the Chinese getting 'cheap popularity', though their fears seem to be exaggerated.

LABEDZ: The Chinese, to return to their side of the argument, are accusing the Russians of betraying the national liberation movement. But could it not be that this is just an ideological smoke-screen to cover China's own narrower nationalist interests?

ADIE: It is hard to sort out the smoke from the fire, for as Mao says, the people—that is, the Maoist Chinese—have one logic and the imperialists another. Maoist logic is emotional and often contradictory. This partly reflects a split within the Chinese Communist Party—its press states that Khrushchev has boasted of having his own good friends among the 'anti-party elements' in the Chinese Communist Party—and partly perhaps it reflects a certain schizophrenia in the minds of individual leaders themselves; they are really not quite sure where analysis of the situation ends and propaganda meant to change it begins. But in view of the party's pre-history of guerrilla warfare, and in view of Mao's own temperament as shown especially in his latest poems, we can assume that they mean what they say when they talk of political power growing out of a rifle barrel or of revolutionary war as an anti-toxin which purges 'both our enemies and ourselves of filth'. This is the Cromwellian approach of a violent prophet possessed of a messianic belief in the need to cleanse a corrupt world by fire and the sword.

Just now the Chinese people are being told they must tighten their belts because two-thirds of the world still remains to be liberated. This argument might sound like a cynical device to justify the rule of an incompetent New Class. But I think it is used with complete sincerity even at high party levels, and certainly at lower ones. In his poem dated January 1963 Mao wrote that time was pressing; 10,000 years are too long to wait; the four seas are in fury and the clouds and water rage. 'Wipe out all vermin till no enemy remains,' he cries. For all the hyperbole, these words have to be taken seriously; Mao really does seem to expect world revolution to sweep away his enemies, especially in Asia, Africa and Latin America.

Now, since the mystique of the Chinese communist régime depends on acceptance of Mao's thought, his party has at least to pretend to believe in revolutionary war and mass struggle as the right *Weltanschauung* in foreign affairs as well as the right instrument for building socialism at home. In the internal construction of China they tried to apply Mao's thought to peaceful tasks. This was the reason for the use of mass movements, and for reliance on the peasants with their simple tools as against the intelligentsia and technical equipment. This was the idea of the 'great leap forward', of the people's communes—an attempt to apply do-it-yourself guerrilla techniques to economics, concentrating unskilled masses on such tasks as steel-making. Though the idea is not entirely wrong, it was carried to an excess that discredited the whole romantic concept of stormy mass movements which underlies Maoism. Now that the Maoist mystique has faded somewhat on the home front, the party tries to prove that it is still valid for the underdeveloped countries.

LABEDZ: The Chinese communists have, from the beginning tended to present their own experiences as a universal model for backward countries to copy. There are two parts to this model—one showing how a communist party can seize power in an underdeveloped country, and the other showing how the party can then develop an agricultural into an industrial economy. The second part of the model has not seemed too encouraging these last years, but the first part still has its attractions to the intelligentsia or semi-intelligentsia. In one respect the Chinese attitude is like Stalin's: it excludes any middle ground between the two world camps. In theory, the Chinese reject the very idea of a 'third world' and say that non-alignment can only be temporary; sooner or later all these new countries must slide down from the fence and join either the 'imperialist' or the 'socialist' camp. When it comes to practice, of course, it is not always clear what these doctrinal pronouncements about 'national democracy' or the 'national bourgeoisie' amount to; the Chinese are as ready to resort to opportunism as the Russians when political or strategic considerations require. Take China's economic aid to the late Imam of Yemen, who was not even a national bourgeois but a benighted feudal lord.

MORISON: I wonder if there is really much difference between the Russians and the Chinese over neutrality. The Russians too, after all, condemn the idea of a 'third world', and when President Nyerere of Tanganyika spoke of a 'second scramble for Africa' and implied that both East and West were involved, the Russians reacted with a very strong article. Both Peking and Moscow seem to accept non-alignment just as long as its spokesmen see no difference between their own positions and the communist ones.

ADIE: As a pupil of Lenin, Mao is, of course, an opportunist and when it suits him he will do a deal with what the Chinese call the 'bourgeois and feudal upper strata'—with a King of Nepal or a King of Morocco; and when the opposite suits him he will promote a 'mass struggle from below'. The respective dosage of united front unity and of united front struggle depends largely on geography. Ideologically the Chinese tend to be tougher toward neutralist leaders, whom they see as so many Chiang Kai-sheks. Although in Africa or Latin America they are more willing than the Russians to see outbreaks of armed struggle, they are more cautious in Asia, where they think escalation might lead to an attack from Formosa or by SEATO forces or both. So even when they decided to fight a limited war against the Indians they made sure of terminating it before it became counter-productive. The Russians think that dealing with the Indian and the Egyptian leaders will pay off in the long run, whereas China has her own reasons to be anti-Indian—such as Tibet. But this Sino-Soviet difference is not really an ideological one so much as a difference in geo-political situation or of national interest pure and simple.

LABEDZ: And what of economic aid?

ADIE: The Chinese are disgusted to see bourgeois Nasser getting so much aid, and Soekarno having more modern Soviet arms than they have. Their own united front experience taught them never to trust Chiang Kai-shek, and they fit Egyptian and Indian leaders into the same pattern. In most cases any special Chinese line can be explained in terms of geography and of China's own history. Peking's policy towards Sihanouk in Cambodia, for example, can be seen in terms of the re-creation of historical links. The present Chinese drive toward Africa and the Mediterranean *via* South-East Asia, Indonesia and Ceylon has precedents in the fifteenth century and earlier.

MORISON: The Soviet attitude to Algeria seems particularly worth noticing. The extreme praise lavished by some Soviet writers on the Ben Bella régime suggests fear that the Chinese could cut the ground there from under their feet. Accordingly the Russians are making special doctrinal accommodations, saying for example that the Algerian rulers are not even a national bourgeoisie but an intelligentsia, albeit possibly of petty-bourgeois origin. Again, though the Russians never say Algeria is advancing toward socialism, they say she is 'on the road to non-capitalist development'. It is hard to believe the Russians would have gone even that far if they had not been afraid of the Chinese courting popularity in Algeria and winning it.

LABEDZ: Though it may have no operative meaning when it comes to political decisions, the doctrinal division between Russians and Chinese over the national bourgeoisie is clear enough. For the Chinese this class is one that is bound sooner or later to betray the national liberation struggle. This is a reflection of the Chinese communists' own experience with Chiang and the Kuomintang in 1927, as Adie has pointed out; and they are fond of referring to other analogies. They are criticizing the Chilean Communist Party, for example, by reminding them of the failure of their policy of cooperation with the Radicals after the assumption of power by Gonzalez Videla in 1947.* The national liberation struggle, the Chinese insist, can only be brought to fruition by the Communist Party on its own.

The Russians, on the other hand, have developed—though not yet perfected—a doctrine of national democracy as a variant of the earlier doctrine of people's democracy. National democracy is to be a sort of half-way house between capitalism and 'socialism', suited to the period between liberation from colonial status and the moment of embarking on the 'road to socialism'. In practical terms it means that the nationalist leaders conduct the anti-colonial struggle while the communists support it and try to penetrate it so as to secure strategic points in the new states in the hope of taking them over at the right time. Of the various countries which the Russians regarded as potential 'states of national democracy' only one, Cuba, has earned the title in the strict sense, while others—Mali, Guinea, Indonesia—have been looked upon as candidates with greater or less optimism as the local winds veered. The Chinese, of course, have taken the pessimistic view that once a nationalist movement consolidates its monopoly of the

* In the September 1964 presidential election, the Popular Front candidate, Salvador Allende, was beaten by the Christian Democratic candidate, Eduardo Frei. The small pro-Chinese communist group in Chile regarded it as a proof that their criticism of the right-wing Party secretary, Luiz Corvalan, was right.

liberation struggle by setting up a one-party system, there will be less possibility than ever of taking power by subversion or penetration.

ADIE: The 'national democracy' formula strikes me as a mere verbal device to cover the Soviet two-stage theory of revolution, with the bourgeoisie allowed to lead in the first stage but the proletariat taking over in the second. It is a riposte to Mao Tse-tung's 'New Democracy' formula, which telescopes the two stages into one continuous revolution. Why do the Russians need two stages? The real question, I feel, is one of controlling the various communist parties. The Soviets want to build up a world economic system of 'socialist' or Soviet Commonwealth—*sodruzhestvo*. This involves a slow process of training revolutionaries from Asia, Africa or Latin America, imbuing them with loyalty to the USSR and some knowledge of Marxism and Leninism, and then sending them back to their own countries to carry out some sort of Gottwald or Rákosi plan, using salami tactics to stage a *coup d'état* rather than a violent revolution, to take over the state machine rather than smash it. With properly trained communists in charge everything is to go on in the normal manner. What a contrast with the 'New Democracy', with the sort of thing that happened in China—and to a certain extent in Yugoslavia—where a mass peasant-nationalist revolt *did* smash the state machine, and then escaped from Soviet control!

We have here two quite different concepts of world revolution: a revolution led by city intellectuals like the original bolsheviks, whose followers have never really mastered the countryside; and on the other hand a Chinese-style peasant revolt in which the countryside, as Mao has often said, surrounds and conquers the cities. The Chinese party veterans are largely peasants, many of them filled with unbounded hatred and mistrust of intellectuals, and inclined toward a primitive egalitarian outlook, especially at the lower levels.

LABEDZ: But in both cases the leaders have surely come from the intelligentsia and semi-intelligentsia. Even Mao, however rural his origin, is not exactly a peasant!

ADIE: Not now, of course. But his father was a rich peasant who exploited the other, poor peasants and Mao, who hated his father, identified himself with them; and he still regards himself as their spokesman although he went to school and read books. He is a sort of populist scholar-warrior in the best Chinese tradition.

MORISON: Reverting to the 'national democracy' formula: this came rather as a bolt from the blue at the 1960 Communist Party Congress.

People wondered whether this was a 'soft' or a 'hard' move. Was it a concession to the national bourgeoisie, to dignify them and make them out to be worthier of communist support than anyone had previously thought? Or was it a move to stiffen the communist parties, to induce greater militance in them and urge them to 'get on top'? The general impression now, I suppose, is that it was a 'hard' move, because at that time there was a general call to reactivate parties, and here was a programme for militant action. . . .

LABEDZ: . . . with what chances of success? Let us consider now whether the Chinese or the Russian tactics for bringing communists into power in the underdeveloped countries are the more promising. The answer will no doubt vary from one region to another; the Chinese method may stand a better chance, say, in Peru than in Chile. Where, in the three great underdeveloped areas of the world, *do* conditions exist which would favour use of peasant guerrilla methods?

MORISON: In Algeria there was a guerrilla movement and a revolution, and despite that there was no communist take-over. In most countries I should have thought that the blueprint for gradual revolution, proposed by the Russians, stood the better chance—but of course it is obvious that the Africans, to take one area, are not going to follow anyone else's 'blueprint' if it is put to them like that. And even if movements owing a lot to communist inspiration and material support have correspondingly greater chances of success, their success would not automatically improve the position of either the communist parties or the communist powers.

LABEDZ: Are you thinking of Zanzibar and the situation in East Africa?

MORISON: That could be an illustration—except that it is so uncertain how far the Russians and Chinese were behind the original Zanzibar *coup* anyway. A revolutionary situation apparently existed on the island—but we know that communist agents in such places sometimes simply hand out money to likely people without their being under specific instructions.

LABEDZ: Does the Middle East offer the Chinese any prospects?

ADIE: The area is quiet at present from their point of view, though in his Cairo communiqué Chou En-lai did make a reference to a practically non-existent struggle in Oman against the British, claiming that

China and Egypt were helping the Omanis. There are also reports of Chinese efforts to split the Syrian Communist Party. This is particularly interesting because most of the exiled Syrian leaders operate from East Germany and Bulgaria.

MORISON: And there is the Jordan waters question, over which the Chinese go further than the Russians in supporting the Arabs against Israel, and that in turn may have been the reason why the Russians declared after the Arab summit conference in Cairo that 'one can sympathize' with the Arab viewpoint.

LABEDZ: And Africa?

ADIE: Chou En-lai says there is an excellent revolutionary situation there, but what he has in mind is the broad prospect of exploiting the movement for African liberation and the armed struggles against the Portuguese and the white South Africans.

LABEDZ: Is there a chance that the Chinese will attempt to promote guerrilla warfare in South Africa?

ADIE: Yes, there are already groups in touch with the Chinese.* Peking's own propaganda at the moment lays much more emphasis on Central than on South Africa. The standard Chinese line makes the point that the Congo produces between 50 and 80 per cent of all uranium used for atomic weapons, and that Africa is vital to the very existence of the European and American capitalist countries. Then, after an attack on neo-colonialism, it usually goes on to say that the people will inevitably rise against the Adoula government and overthrow it. An article along these lines appeared in the *Peking Review* of 10 January 1964—just two days before the Zanzibar *coup*; near the end of the same month the *People's Daily* carried an article hailing the revolt in the Congolese province of Kwilu, which was led by Pierre Mulele, a man trained in Peking and only back in Africa since July 1963. After that another rising broke out in the province of Kivu, bordering on Tanganyika.

This sort of thing hardly seems like an accident. I should guess that the Chinese in Dar Es-Salaam had been looking forward to the time when they could send in help and supplies to the Lumumbists in the

* At a Peking rally in April 1964 a Chinese spokesman hailed the armed struggle in Pondoland and called for more in very violent terms. Later, in Peking, Oginga Odinga of Kenya demanded Chinese aid in a war against South Africa, but the Chinese News Agency censored this part of his speech.

Congo, in the present case to Mulele. In 1960 and 1961 the Chinese had requests for aid from the Lumumbists and from Gizenga—they accuse the Russians, of course, of letting those people down, and allowing Lumumba himself to be killed—but at that time Tanganyika stood in the way.

The most urgent motive for Chinese intriguing in Zanzibar and Tanganyika would be the laying of a 'pipeline' of assistance to the Lumumbists; there is in fact a railway leading up to a lake on the Congo frontier. But the obvious time to act would be *after* the final withdrawal of UN troops from the Congo. So it looks as if the East African troubles of 1963 went off prematurely from the Chinese point of view.

LABEDZ: What about the Portuguese territories in Africa?

ADIE: An uprising is reportedly planned for Mozambique; that is what they are all plotting in Dar Es-Salaam. Certain Pan-Africanists are getting help from Algeria and probably from the Chinese too; the Chinese News Agency stated that the first arms shipment from Algeria arrived in Tanganyika on 7 January 1964. The plan is supposed to be that Angola and Mozambique will be liberated first; then southern Rhodesia; and only then will it be time to start in South Africa; there must be unbroken lines of communication throughout. However, I doubt if they will stick to this plan and, as Morison says, this is the kind of situation where agents are handing out arms and money with or without the knowledge of their sponsoring governments, and have little control of the situation, or even of their *protégés*.

We were previously discussing the rival attractions of the Russian and Chinese models. The Russian model depends a great deal on the idea of the returned student, and the Lumumba University in Moscow is going to send back its trainees to Africa in particular. The Chinese, of course, are bound to recall that in their own country the returned bolsheviks made an appalling mess of the revolution until Mao took over. But I suspect that the Zanzibar *coup* indicates that events in the underdeveloped countries are likely to disappoint communists of both colours: the Arab nationalists there, the Chinese protégé Babu, and the Russian protégé Hanga, were all outwitted—in the first phase at least—by that thoroughly African free-booter Okello. Later Okello lost his grip, but anything might still happen in Zanzibar and the returned students from Russia and China alike may turn out, in these revolutionary African situations, to be rejected in the end by the local revolutionary forces.

LABEDZ: Or again they may be disillusioned before they even return —like the Ghanaians in Moscow.

ADIE: And by all the evidence some Ghanaians and other Africans have been just as unhappy in Peking as in Moscow. The cultural differences, after all, are extreme, and African students have often interpreted incidents arising from them as if they were due to racialism and paternalism.

MORISON: The Chinese have no doubt overdone the argument that they are 'coloured', since it is so easy to reply that they are not black; but I wonder if they do not gain in the eyes of the 'third world', if anyone is comparing them with the Russians, from their ability to present themselves as historically 'underdogs'. Compared with them, the Russians have been 'top dogs' for quite a time now and have much more of a great-power aura than the Chinese.

LABEDZ: Historically, though, Chinese underdog status does not go back beyond the nineteenth century.

ADIE: And I think any contact with real, live Chinese communists should eventually dispel whatever prejudice Africans might have in their favour based on woolly ideas of 'Afro-Asian solidarity'.

LABEDZ: We have not yet touched on Latin America. The tactics advocated for that continent by Castro, and especially by his chief theoretician Ché Guevara, resemble those of China. Are they identical, and can we expect the Chinese to play any substantial role here?

ADIE: Certainly a substantial propaganda role. They look upon all Latin America as a second 'centre of world storms' alongside the main centre, Africa. Recently the *Peking Review* printed a long article by Ché Guevara, explaining far more clearly and frankly than the Chinese have ever done the whole mechanics of seizing power by guerrilla warfare—regardless of the original state of mind of the populace. He shows how you can provoke a government into taking repressive measures and so turn the people against it, even if they were not in the least revolutionary-minded to begin with.

The Cubans have said that it is mere accident that their views coincide with those of the Chinese. But I think the real reason for the 'coincidence' emerges clearly from Ché Guevara's remark that if the revolution is not intensified it may move backward. This, he adds, is why guerrilla warfare must spread throughout Latin America, though it may cost much blood.

That is the sort of sentiment the Chinese like to hear. In the same issue of *Peking Review* they printed a series of short news items about new armed struggles in various Latin American countries, all to illustrate Mao's well-known dictum that 'one spark can start a prairie fire'. Over-simplifying somewhat, one might say that the Cubans and Chinese share the basic anxiety to intensify the revolution for fear of it moving backward, though they see the framework differently. The Chinese have a genuine fear of a counter-revolutionary come-back because of their domestic difficulties and their inability to deal with Chiang Kai-shek. The Cubans for their part simply need the revolution to spread to Latin America because their country is hardly viable on its own.

LABEDZ: I suspect that the Chinese have themselves misjudged the Latin American situation. There are of course Castro-ite elements outside Cuba—among intelligentsia, peasantry, the miners in Bolivia—but there is a well-developed middle class in several of the republics, and there are democratic political institutions in countries like Chile. In the one country where they have tried the Castro tactics, Venezuela, they have not been particularly successful even in provoking the government into repressions. Despite the guerrilla activity of the National Liberation Front, Bétancourt was succeeded by President Leoni in a regular election. Their failure has led to a split in the Liberation Front between the Venezuelan Communist Party proper and the left-wing socialist MIR (Movement of the Revolutionary Left), the latter enjoying increasing support from Moscow, while the Communist Party continues to represent the militant line of Peking and Castro. But the Cuban communists themselves depend on Soviet aid and so are inhibited from going full steam ahead with their own preferred tactics in Latin America. In other places local communists generally prefer the slow methods of penetration because they have had long experience of failure with revolutionary tactics in the 'twenties, 'thirties and even 'forties. This creates a situation in which the militants tend to split off. Thus in Brazil we now have two communist parties, while in Peru the pro-Chinese wing has taken over the party. But though there may be dissatisfaction in several Latin American communist parties, and the Chinese may be exploiting it for their own propaganda, I very much doubt if there is a greater likelihood of a successful communist *coup* anywhere thanks to the use of Chinese tactics.

But now I should like to broach a further point: how far does economic aid given by the Russians and the East Europeans on the one hand, and by the Chinese on the other, enhance the chances of local communists? Is there a difference in economic strategy?

MORISON: The first point I would make is that Russia, by giving great economic aid to a given country, immediately acquires a vested interest in that country's stability. The Chinese make rude remarks about Soviet aid and accuse the Russians of seeking joint imperialist exploitation of the underdeveloped countries. But within their capacity they are engaging in quite a lot of economic aid themselves, and as it increases, so, I should think, would their own interest in the stability of the recipient countries.

My second point is that economic aid is always a hostage to fortune. You help a country like Iraq, and then it persecutes its communists. There was a veiled threat that Russia would withdraw aid from Iraq—but nothing came of it.

LABEDZ: And the same has happened in Nasser's Egypt and elsewhere. But I am not sure about your formula of a vested interest in the recipient's stability.

ADIE: I should say that the aim of Soviet economic aid is not to produce political stability but to create such changes in the economic structure of a country as would be followed, according to Marxism, by certain changes in the social structure too. You will have central planning, state trading agencies and so on, with either Soviet-trained natives, or actual Soviet citizens or agents, as experts in some key points. With their help these countries will gradually become more and more like one of the states of the USSR; as the economic system tends to become the same, so will the social system. Afghanistan, for example, is supposed to get more and more like Kazakhstan.

MORISON: The Russians themselves claim that aid from their bloc will promote the development of the state sector and the emergence of the most 'progressive' elements in society.

ADIE: But is this revolutionary justification of economic aid always a sincere one? Are not some Soviet officials, at least, simply in favour of trade because they want to improve the living standards of their own people, and not just engage in economic competition with the West?

MORISON: I agree that the 'revolutionary content' of aid is exaggerated by the Russians. How far they believe in the revolutionary effectiveness of aid is one thing; how far it *is* effective—in their sense—is another. For myself I regard the whole trend toward economic assistance of the underdeveloped countries as one that promotes stability and is thus to be welcomed, whatever source it comes from, even if there are ulterior motives in some cases which we do not approve.

ADIE: Coming to economic aid from China, so far the Chinese have not had much to give. Up to 1962 China's aid to all African and Asian countries together was about the same as Czechoslovakia's, or roughly a tenth of the bloc total. When Peking has finished paying off her debts to Moscow in 1965, there may be more to offer. But I doubt whether this aid has affected local communist parties much in the sense of determining their choice in the Sino-Soviet issue—it has simply given them the means to recruit agents and infiltrate organizations.

LABEDZ: To sum up so far, then: we have considered the impact of the Sino-Soviet dispute on the underdeveloped countries in three main aspects. One was the issue of non-alignment; another was the controversy over gradualist versus revolutionary tactics; a third was that of economic aid. Do these factors tend to combine or to cancel out?

ADIE: The Russians have, of course, infinitely more to offer by way of aid, and this, plus other factors like stability and international responsibility, must appeal in countries where development has gone a little way. But in really underdeveloped places like the Congo, Chinese militancy—bow-and-arrow warfare and so on—is far more attractive to hot-heads than any 'intellectual' merits in the Soviet pattern.

LABEDZ: But we must also consider a fourth aspect of the Sino-Soviet differences—the way in which they affect the growth of polycentrism.

ADIE: Yes, I think an essential feature of the Chinese method of revolution is that it does not primarily produce communists, but national communists or, one might say, national socialists! And the system likely to emerge from Chinese-style revolution is neither socialism nor communism but simply a para-military dictatorial revolutionary régime like that of Kassem in Iraq. Such régimes do not form an ideological bloc, except on paper and on the air. Now, in view of the past decade, can one say that the Russian method, using gradualist tactics and placing faith in 'intellectual attraction', has been or is likely to be any more successful in producing régimes loyal to a unified socialist camp? It has not stopped polycentrism even amongst régimes formally committed to Marxism; among the new countries there seems even less reason for an intelligentsia, an élite, a revolutionary group to tie itself specifically to any one model.

MORISON: The very existence of a dispute between the Russians and the Chinese is spoiling the chances of either of them imposing their own specific brand of communism. The respective images of the two countries, so far as they can be detached from communism, are probably as popular or unpopular as before. But the dispute discredits the ideology and makes it easier for Africans and Asians to disentangle that aspect from the national one. They can see that aid is a good thing, but without doctrine, thank you. I think they will say that more and more, as these verbal exchanges pile up.

LABEDZ: So much, then, for our fourth and last point—polycentrism. Whereas the first three factors we looked at were inconclusive, favouring now the Russians, now the Chinese, according to the type of underdeveloped country under consideration, this last aspect of the Sino-Soviet rift goes against both communist giants. Marxist states are not supposed to have rifts, and no communist spokesman can even start explaining the reasons to an African or Asian without abandoning the aura of dogmatic unity that used to be such an asset to him. He speaks no longer *ex cathedra*, but *ex parte*, not a high priest, but a barrister. And to an increasing extent his advice and his ideological urgings, like his offers of material aid, may come to be looked upon with the same healthy scepticism to which western representatives have long since accustomed themselves.

6

The Parties in the West

SPEAKERS

G. F. Hudson

David Floyd

Leopold Labedz

6. The Parties in the West

LABEDZ: We will have to make a distinction here at the outset: we have in western Europe two firmly established communist parties—the Italian and the French—which are forces to be reckoned with in the political life of their countries, with a real—if slightly remote—chance of gaining power some day. The Italian communists now hold about 25 per cent of the seats in parliament. On the other hand, we have the small parties in Britain, Scandinavia, Belgium, and elsewhere which I would classify under the heading of 'political *curiosa*' rather than 'political power'. To begin with the two big parties: how is the domestic position of the Italian Party likely to be affected by the disappearance of a single unchallenged centre of world communism?

HUDSON: We can look at the impact of the split on the Italian as well as the French Party in two ways, for it could have positive *or* negative consequences for these parties. The question is: which will ultimately carry greater weight. The negative consequence would be the undermining of the purity of their ideological position. If you no longer have a single unchallenged centre of world communism but you have two great parties in power with diametrically opposed official dogmas, then you eliminate what has always been one of the most appealing features of communism for many people in search of a lay, 'ersatz' religion—its ability to answer convincingly *all* essential questions in the framework of an all-embracing theology. But the positive consequence of the Sino-Soviet split may well be that, by encouraging and contributing to the growing autonomy of the different national communist parties, it may give them the strength that comes from acquiring local roots, from having a strategy and tactics that are more in line with the requirements of their particular local situation. Togliatti has probably been acutely aware of the great importance of this kind of adaptation to local needs for quite some time, and no doubt it was one of the main ideas at the back of his now famous concept of polycentrism.

FLOYD: I would agree that all the changes that have taken place since 1956, and above all the split between China and the Soviet Union, have thrown the West European communist leaders back on their own resources. They can no longer lean back and turn to the Kremlin for instructions; they have to come to grips with local politics. This, of course, helps to free them from one of the greatest handicaps under which all the western communist parties have laboured in the past—the odium of being mere agents of a foreign power, with all the tortuous changes in the local party line which that involved. But I am not so sure that this will necessarily make things easier for them. It will mean that they will have to enter into agreements and understandings with other political parties of the left—as, in fact, they are already doing, and this, in turn, will water down the revolutionary programme. They will cease to be communist parties in the sense in which they were in the days of Stalin.

LABEDZ: If we are to believe Luigi Longo, this will not happen. At the last Party Congress he said that the growing autonomy of the Italian communists was not leading to a dilution of the revolutionary message.

He asserted that it was the Chinese understanding of Marx that was static because it was not taking into account changes in the 'objective' situation. The question we have to ask ourselves is whether, in the long run, we can envisage a transformation of the Italian party—which is, after all, at the extreme right in the political spectrum of the international communist movement—into something which could be integrated into the democratic framework of the Italian Republic. Obviously this could only be a long-term process in which all kinds of difficulties would have to be overcome: can we see any indications that such a process is under way at all?

HUDSON: As the largest of the communist parties in Europe outside the communist-governed countries, the Italian Party has perhaps the best prospects of reaching power in a coalition of the left through parliamentary means. This means a revival in some form of 'popular front' tactics, such as were used in the Stalin period in western Europe in the 'thirties. It means that the Communist Party must acquire a respectable image in the eyes of the general public, that it must have flexibility of political manœuvre to enable it to strike bargains with the Italian socialists, and even with left-wing liberal elements, so that it might come to power as part of a coalition.

This seems to be the ultimate purpose of Khrushchev's own line since the 20th Congress. It need not mean a genuine conversion to democracy, because communists can, once they have acquired levers of power, use them to oust their coalition partners, but it does mean that they should use tactics of moderation and abstain from obviously revolutionary tactics. Given the facts that the Italians have the largest communist party in western Europe and that Italian politics are decidedly unstable, this may very well be their best bet. Therefore I think that, although now the most revisionist west European party, the Italian Communist Party is still, or perhaps because of it, fundamentally in accordance with Khrushchev's line for the parties of western Europe.

LABEDZ: ... Which is, of course, ample reason for the Chinese communists to oppose it so strongly. We have been hearing a great deal lately about the influence of Chinese propaganda on dissidents within the Italian Party. But do they really represent a serious problem for the Italian communist leaders?

FLOYD: The pro-Chinese element in Italy is not even particularly vocal, much less influential. There is a very small group of pro-Chinese communists who publish the mimeographed sheet *Ritorniamo a Lenin!*,* but its influence on Italian politics is nil, and I rather suspect that its influence within the party can be easily exaggerated. More serious, to my mind, is the frustration of the kind of revolutionary impulse which is impatient with these subtle tactics of Togliatti, with the so-called 'structural reform' and other gradualist improvements.

LABEDZ: So far, such frustration has, curiously enough, found more vocal expression among the socialists, as we can see from the split which occurred in the Italian Socialist Party, whose right wing, headed by Nenni, has been ready to cooperate with the Christian Democrats and is now part of the government. This led the left-wing socialists, headed by Tullio Vecchietti, to break away and found the 'Italian Socialist Party of Proletarian Unity'.

HUDSON: Here the attitude of the Italian communists deserves special attention. Togliatti was not at all pleased with the socialist split, even though the party organ could do nothing but pay lip-service approval and express solidarity with the new Socialist Party. Why? Some of the socialist left-wingers who were in full sympathy with the communist party had acquired important strategic positions in the *old* Socialist Party. To a great extent, these people had been able to control and influence the Socialist Party's policy between congresses, and now this lever of influence is largely gone. The left-wing socialists who were planning for unity of action with the communists are no longer in the party, leaving in control the right-wingers who envisage co-operation with the Christian Democrats in government.

* It ceased to appear in 1964 and a new pro-Chinese publication, *Nuova Unità*, began to appear.

LABEDZ: Yes, the *Carristi* are gone, yet the Nenni socialists cannot do the logical thing and unite with the Saragat Social Democrats, because 'centrists' like Ricardo Lombardi oppose it.

We should pause here for a moment to examine a little more closely Hudson's argument that the Italian communists' policy is 'fundamentally in accordance with Khrushchev's line for the West European parties'. What, specifically, is Khrushchev's line?

HUDSON: I think Khrushchev's idea is that if communist parties formed alliances of the 'popular front' type, combining, for example, with pacifist organizations, and if they could then obtain sufficient influence in west European countries, this could break up NATO, and would pull the west European countries away from America and in fact change their foreign policies. Naturally, it is possible that if they became revisionist and autonomous enough, they might even turn into parties which wanted to stay in NATO—one cannot be quite sure about that. But, at any rate, I believe that Khrushchev conceives of his policy for the west European communists as something which could help the Soviet Union by disrupting NATO. He had, probably by 1956, come to the conclusion that these were the proper tactics, recognizing that there were no prospects of communist seizures of power in western Europe.

LABEDZ: But can we actually reduce the problem to what *Khrushchev* envisages as the proper tactics for the west European parties?

FLOYD: No, I don't think we can do this any longer because the Italian Communist Party has been taking certain lines which do not coincide with what Khrushchev wants or envisages for them. The approach to the Common Market is a good illustration of this. Khrushchev has clearly been very much afraid of the development of the Common Market and has done everything he could to disrupt it. The manifest need for more trade with the Market countries may be gradually leading him to revise his attitude now, but the Soviet Union has to this day refused to recognize the existence of the Market diplomatically. The Italian Communist Party, on the other hand, has taken, if not a positive attitude toward the Six, at least a line which acknowledges that this is a development to which the party will have to adjust itself. Here we have a clear-cut clash between the Soviet and the Italian Party's attitude on a vital question of west European life.

LABEDZ: And also a clash between that of the Italian and the French parties. What are the important questions on which the Italian and French communists differ?

HUDSON: Apart from the Common Market problem, where Thorez has closely followed the Moscow line—as he has indeed notably succeeded in doing over the past thirty years—the French have a different attitude towards de-Stalinization itself. The third, and perhaps most interesting, issue is that of the tactics to be adopted with respect to the Chinese. Now, both parties agree in substance with the Soviet line on peaceful coexistence and the rest, but, for their own reasons, come to quite different conclusions as to the proper tactics to be adopted *vis-à-vis* the Chinese party. Both in the autumn of 1963, when Khrushchev first toyed with the idea of holding an international conference of the communist parties to deal with the Chinese deviation, and later, when he was pressing even more insistently for such a conference to condemn the heresy, the French gave him their full, outspoken support. The Italian Communist Party was among those whose opposition made Khrushchev reconsider and repeatedly postpone the implementation of the idea, and they have come out clearly and openly against holding a conference. At the same time it seems rather ironical that the 'revisionist', more right-wing, if you will, Italian Party is so much opposed to the public pronouncement of anathema against the Chinese at an international conference.

LABEDZ: But isn't this quite understandable from the point of view of the well-considered self-interest of the Italian Party?

HUDSON: Yes, of course, and if we needed any further proof of this, we now have it in Togliatti's own words. In many of his statements on the Sino-Soviet conflict, he emphasized the autonomy and sovereignty of each party as prerequisites for the development of the movement, and then had something like this to say: 'The method of solemn excommunication is dangerous because it may revive the authoritarian and sectarian streak in the leadership of each party.' A veteran leader like Togliatti has no doubt vivid enough memories of the Comintern, the Cominform and the excommunication of Yugoslavia in 1948 to know what he is talking about, and he may also be aware that at another time and under different circumstances the victim of excommunication might be the revisionist Italian Party itself.

LABEDZ: From this tug-of-war in the European communist movement on the question of an international conference I would go one step further. In my opinion, it shows that the whole development in recent years, culminating in the Sino-Soviet rift, has led to a rather important change in the nature of the relationship between the Soviet Union and the western parties. The latter now have to be regarded by Moscow, not as tools which can be manipulated at will, but as much-needed allies. With the struggle against Peking on its hands, Moscow needs the support of the big west European parties as much as they need the ultimate power of Russia. It has to woo these parties, take their local requirements into consideration, and, if need be, bow to their pressure.

FLOYD: The withdrawal in March 1964 of the anti-semitic booklet published by the Ukrainian Academy of Sciences after all major western parties had protested against this work—something which the needs of their image at home no doubt compelled them to do—is a good case in point.

LABEDZ: This is an act that would have been very unlikely even a few years ago. But let us now take a closer look at the reasons for these striking differences between the French and Italian parties which have, as far as their general situation and standing are concerned, a good deal in common. What has made these two parties so different in their reactions to the split?

FLOYD: My feeling here is that a good deal of that difference is due to what the Chinese call 'style'. One cannot avoid the impression that Togliatti has a very much better 'style' than Thorez and his colleagues.* The Italian leaders are more skilful. They appear to be more aware of what is taking place in European politics, they are more sophisticated in making their approaches to other parties, more subtle, less rigidly Stalinist than the French. In their handling of their internal affairs, there is probably no party more Stalinist than the French, no matter how much they may back Moscow's anti-Peking line, and themselves accuse the Peking leadership of Stalinism.

LABEDZ: Togliatti is indeed a remarkable phenomenon, embodying, as he does the flexibility of that curious Italian phenomenon: the political *combinazione*.

FLOYD: And though he was personally implicated in the crimes of the Stalin era—not having had the good fortune of being imprisoned in Mussolini's Italy, as some of the present Italian leaders were—he is basically not a purely Stalinist type, as far as his personality and the political tradition behind him are concerned.

* In May 1964, at the 17th Congress of the French party, Waldeck Rochet replaced Thorez as the Secretary-General. In July 1964 Thorez died, and five weeks later came the death of Togliatti. He was succeeded by Luigi Longo.

This is not the only factor which explains these differences in 'style'. We can see a new type of cadre emerging in Italy. The old-style Stalinist *apparatchiks* are now in their sixties, and new, more business-like cadres are coming to the fore, particularly in such communist strongholds as Reggio Emilia. They have no influence on party policy so far, because they have no representatives in the politburo and very few in the central committee, but at the same time they have been remarkably successful in local elections and in local government. In Bologna they have established cooperatives which are run along the line of Yugoslav enterprises, that is, with cost accounting and business methods. One could say that a kind of communist *apparatchik* in grey flannels is gradually emerging.

LABEDZ: This would seem to suggest that the Italian communists do have forces at their disposal which would enable them to succeed in carrying out a more pragmatic programme, in better adapting themselves to local conditions. But has there been any comparable development in the French party?

HUDSON: I don't think there has. The French Party suffers, as it has suffered in the past, from an old-fashioned leadership which is very rigid in its policies. The Stalinist *apparatchiks* from Thorez on down were already leading the party in the 'thirties, and the party has become frozen in its attitudes. This has led to a situation where the French intellectuals have left the party—or been expelled from it—and where the channels of advancement of the new generation have been blocked. This is precisely the kind of situation which we don't have, by and large, in the Italian Communist Party. One expression of this frustration was the revolt, in 1963, of the communist students in France. The 'anti-party' forces won, and the leadership of the Communist Students' Union was seized by the revisionists. In 1964 the party has been trying to reach a compromise, under which the rebels joined forces with the 'pro-party' men, and they were being opposed by a curious coalition of right-wing revisionists and pro-Chinese elements. These rumblings beneath the surface might be a portent of things to come within the party itself. An underground 'Italian' tendency is clearly in the making.

FLOYD: There is one other factor we have to bear in mind: the pro-Chinese or dogmatist element in France has now been given a certain impetus by the official policy of the French Government. One of the consequences of de Gaulle's recognition of Communist China has been that the extremely militant magazine first printed in Lausanne in French and English, under the title of *Revolution*—it has on its cover Asia, Africa, and Latin America and is addressed particularly to Africans—has now begun to be distributed from Paris under the eyes of the French police. There will presumably be some distribution of this magazine in the states of the former French African empire. Whether de Gaulle quite likes this kind of development one cannot tell, but at any rate these new relations between France and China have indirect effects on the French movement. Also, France remains much more closely involved in the Afro-Asian world than Italy, which is now almost completely detached from ex-colonial affairs.

HUDSON: The pro-Chinese elements among the communists in France are more significant than they are in Italy, because they appeal to the traditional French type of Bohemian intellectual who must have some sort of a revolutionary image to worship, and therefore Castro or Ché Guevara or Mao or any forthcoming romantic figure of a revolutionary leader will be bound to appeal to his sentiments.

LABEDZ: In 1956 the Italian party had a total of 2,200,000 members, and now there are only 1,600,000—a loss of more than half a million. After the war the French Party had almost 900,000 members, now it has probably no more than a quarter of a million. But this drop in membership has by no means affected the electoral appeal of the parties. Earlier I mentioned the successes achieved by the Italian communists at the last general elections. Well, in the recent (March 1964) local elections in France, the Communist Party also made substantial gains. This would appear to show that people vote for these parties for reasons which are completely unconnected with de-Stalinization and the Sino-Soviet dispute.

FLOYD: This may also suggest that the growing autonomy of the west European mass communist parties is contributing to their electoral appeal, at the same time as the ideological dissension is contributing to a fall in membership.

HUDSON: Yes, and I would also say that, as far as France is concerned, even though the present influence of the Sino-Soviet rift on the domestic political scene seems a good deal less important than that exercised on the Italian party, the French communists have rather good prospects of recovering their influence. De Gaulle's great popularity, extending even to the French working class, was, after all, due to the image of him as the man who extricated France from the Algerian war; but this is only a temporary popularity which may decline, while the traditional prestige of the Communist Party with the French workers may revive.

LABEDZ: Coming to the small west European parties, what kind of an impact is the Sino-Soviet split having on the communist parties in such places as Britain, Belgium and Scandinavia?

FLOYD: For one thing, I think that in these countries, where the communists' prospects of gaining power are so remote, the issues in the dispute—which have been couched mainly in ideological terms both by the Russians and the Chinese—really do begin to take on greater significance.

LABEDZ: There you can indulge in questions of ideological purity, and dispute the issues to your heart's content, while in France and Italy, where the communist parties have to deal with practical questions, they cannot afford to concentrate on them...

FLOYD: ... and for the small parties this kind of activity is a substitute for engaging in real politics. Take Britain: I am quite sure that people like Palme Dutt have a genuine leaning towards the Chinese. When Peking puts out one of its statements which rings of the good honest Stalinizm of the past, I think it must touch the heart strings of a Palme Dutt. There is also one other point: the Sino-Soviet conflict is a convenient device for fighting your opponents, whether or not you hold particularly strong views about it. In various small parties where personal struggles for leadership are going on, this conflict must seem almost heaven-sent, because it provides you with a stick to beat the other man with.

LABEDZ: This would certainly seem to be the case in Belgium where we now have two communist parties, a pro-Chinese and a pro-Soviet. The pro-Chinese Party is centred on the Brussels Federation, headed by Jacques Grippa, a veteran communist who has been openly critical of the 'peaceful coexistence' line ever since the 22nd Congress.

HUDSON: Actually, what we have been witnessing in Belgium is rather of the order of comic opera than of serious politics—it is a microcosm of the Sino-Soviet dispute carried *ad absurdum*. In Brussels we actually have *two* communist federations now, each claiming the sole right to legitimacy. When, in the spring of 1963, the Grippa group was expelled at the Belgian Party Congress for its 'factional' activity, the group promptly held its own Brussels federation congress, and expelled its own expellers, condemning them as 'revisionists'. This, of course, is a petty family quarrel which is not of particularly great interest to the Belgian political community as a whole, for neither of the parties—federation à la Moscow or federation à la Peking—has much chance of influencing the general political situation.

FLOYD: I think that regardless of the strength, or rather, weakness, of the Belgian communists at the present time, these internal developments are of some general significance. This is the first case in western Europe where the Sino-Soviet split has caused—or at least helped—the emergence of a rival party. And beyond this, we can see that Peking itself is very closely involved in the factionalism of the Belgian Party. Visits have been made by dissident leaders to both Peking and Tirana, and in the spring of 1963 the Chinese news agency *Hsinhua* opened an office in Brussels, with a Grippa man in charge, and it has been most active ever since. This development may be a sign of things to come in other small western parties.

LABEDZ: There is a further point here; the split not only places a useful weapon into the hands of the small party leaders for fighting out their personal feuds: the smaller the party, the greater the temptation to magnify its own part in the dispute by trying to play the role of honest broker. A minute ago we spoke of Palme Dutt as a kind of crypto-Chinese sympathizer. I think we should also mention John Gollan, who has been very pro-Soviet, but nevertheless went to Peking at the beginning of 1963 and has been trying to inflate the political role of the British Communist Party out of all proportion to its actual domestic influence.

FLOYD: Quite unsuccessfully, as has been the case with all such attempts. I would prefer to stress not the opportunities which the split may offer these weak West European parties, but rather their embarrassment and concern with it. In Scandinavia the split, with all the factionalism it brings out into the open, comes at a time when the Scandinavian communist parties are continuing to lose in their electoral appeal. For some time now they have been facing the serious challenge of left-wing socialism, which threatens to take away a good part of the communists' traditional electoral clientele. In both Denmark and Norway, the left-wing socialists have already succeeded in doing serious damage to the communists. All the Scandinavian parties are aware that they will have to change their public image if they are to halt or even slow down the decline, that they too must inevitably become more flexible, less Moscow-oriented—in a word, more 're-visionist'. The replacement of the veteran Swedish Stalinist leader Hagberg was an indication of this.

HUDSON: Nor is this all: those who would give Scandinavian communism a modern look have also to contend with suspicion and a total lack of understanding of new-fangled ideas on the part of many of the old leaders. These leaders are so steeped in the dogmatic self-complacency that comes from being removed from the seats of political power that they now appear impervious to change.

LABEDZ: In short, for the communist parties of Scandinavia the Sino-Soviet split has further complicated a situation that was already difficult enough.

FLOYD: Yes, and this appears to be reflected in their indecisive behaviour towards the two great contesting communist powers. In each of their statements one can sense how peeved they are by it all and can discern an inclination to say 'A plague on both your houses!'

LABEDZ: We have been talking so far only about communist parties, big and small; but the split is, of course, both a family quarrel, and —like most family quarrels—also much more than that because it can profoundly affect the everyday life of the neighbours. So, turning to the implications of the Sino-Soviet split for the states of western Europe, the enigma and highly fascinating case of de Gaulle again comes to mind, since he has been the first western politician to draw his own conclusions from the conflict and translate them into action— by which I am, of course, referring to the French recognition of the Peking government. What basic political objectives does de Gaulle have in mind?

HUDSON: De Gaulle would like to see a stronger China. I think he considers that this could do no real harm to French interests, because these have been eliminated from East Asia in any case, but that it might divert the interest and power of the Soviet Union. Broadly speaking, de Gaulle's objective is to create a third force in western Europe which can stand up to Russia without being dependent on the United States. Of course, in terms of real power the Soviet Union is still so very much the strongest state in Europe that this is a difficult thing to achieve, even with a *force de frappe*. But the Chinese have an obvious nuisance value from the French point of view, because they can make trouble for Russia in Asia, and the more trouble they can make, the more the Russians will have to devote attention to Asian affairs, instead of concentrating on their policies in Europe.

This is de Gaulle's long-term view of the situation. The recognition of Communist China was, I think, very carefully prepared and thought out, and though it was obviously designed to annoy Washington, that was not the whole of its purpose. Nor do I think that the economic advantages which may or may not accrue from it were decisive considerations for de Gaulle. I believe he thinks primarily in terms of creating a new balance of power in the world, that he does not attach great importance to ideological differences, and that he considers that —in a roundabout way—Communist China could be a very useful aid to French foreign policy.

LABEDZ: But how would this influence Franco-Soviet relations? There is also the possibility of a warming up of Franco-Soviet relations. Does this not clash with the assumption that de Gaulle's China policy is directed against Russia in the crude sense of balancing one against the other?

FLOYD: I am not at all sure that the balance of power can be upset by any move on the part of Paris. I think the balance of power is fundamentally a balance of power between Moscow and Washington, and I do not think the *force de frappe* or any French *rapprochement* with Peking can make a great deal of difference.

LABEDZ: We are talking about the balance of power in the political, and not just in the military sense.

FLOYD: Yes, but to me, this talk of looking towards Peking or Moscow does not seem to get at the essence of the matter. What is most important here is that we are going to see the formation of a separate centre in the Far East. This is certainly going to be more important than any upsetting of the NATO.

LABEDZ: At any rate, we are witnessing a growing autonomy of the centres of power, whether in China or in western Europe. How will the latter influence the old alignment of forces in the West?

HUDSON: Khrushchev's attempt to project a new image of the Soviet Union and the idea of peaceful coexistence has already had a certain effect in loosening the bonds of NATO and of the relations between western states. For it was precisely the fear of Russian coercion or aggression that brought NATO into being and maintained it as an active force as long as that sense of danger from Russia existed. Insofar as it diminishes and France and other countries adopt more independent policies, the western grouping comes apart. To some extent this development runs parallel with the division between Russia and China in the communist camp. Things could change again, of course, if new international crises arose, if the Russians did something provocative in Europe, or if there was a new clash between America and China. But the world-trend is towards polycentrism, towards a loosening of ties in *both* blocs.

As for de Gaulle's relations with the Soviet Union, there are signs, as you say, of a warming up of these relations, but I don't think this is in contradiction with his tactics of a *rapprochement* with Peking. This makes him more valuable from the Russian point of view. His price goes up, and it will be more important for Russia to try and establish good relations with France if France is becoming more independent and a greater power in the world, and this is what de Gaulle has been trying to make her.

LABEDZ: In other words, we have polycentrism both East and West. But—and here is the main difference—polycentrism in the West has no 'theological framework', for we are held together not by ideology and a common movement, but by a thousand less obvious ties. It is therefore less dangerous for the coherence of the West than it is for that of the East. As to the communist parties, both East and West, they are just beginning to discover the limits of freedom within which they can operate in the new setting.

7

The Ramifications of the
Split in the Parties
and Front Organizations

SPEAKERS

Alfred Sherman

Kevin Devlin

Leopold Labedz

7. The Ramifications of the Split in Parties and Front Organizations

LABEDZ: Factionalism is not a new phenomenon in the history of the movements which derive from Marx. Doctrinal organizations have always had a tendency to propagate by fission. However, during the thirty years of Stalin's rule factionalism was in decline—that is, the autocracy of Stalin, and the fact that the USSR was the only communist state, imposed upon the foreign communist parties a sort of monolithic unity which was not as complete or genuine as it seemed, but was nevertheless effective. The heretics were expelled; they had no chance to act within the parties.

This state of affairs seems to have ended with the Sino-Soviet split. At the moment there is hardly a country outside the bloc which can boast of the existence of a communist party without an 'anti-party' faction or group or tendency, or even a publication. In some countries the pro-Chinese forces have even succeeded in taking over a formerly pro-Soviet party or establishing a rival party. Over the past year or so this process has been accelerating, both inside the parties and in the front organizations.

I should like to begin by advancing a general proposition, or raising a general question, about just what sort of phenomenon we are dealing with. I think one can perhaps draw a parallel between the Sino-Soviet conflict and the struggle between the Guelphs and the Ghibellines, Empire versus Papacy, in twelfth-century Europe. Like all historical parallels, it cannot be taken too far, or even very far; the differences are obvious. But there is one element they all have in common—the way in which local conflicts become more intense because of the existence of the great central conflict, and become connected with it or identified with it. Just as local clashes of interest in medieval Italy eventually resolved themselves in terms of Papacy versus Empire, so today local communist antagonisms, which would otherwise have remained latent as in Stalin's time, are sharpened by the Sino-Soviet dispute and tend to find expression in terms of that dispute. The question is whether this tendency is leading to a bipolarization of the communist movement—one church with its centre in Moscow, so to speak, and the other with its centre in Peking—or whether, because of this general loosening of the old bonds, each communist party will tend to determine its attitude not primarily by its allegiance to Moscow or Peking, the contemporary Guelphs and Ghibellines of the communist world, but by self-interest. In other words, how far are we dealing here with a schism between *two* centres, and how far with a process leading to polycentrism, the creation of further centres of power, or at least, to a greater autonomy of the communist parties *vis-à-vis* either of the centres?

SHERMAN: There is something of both involved. I agree with what you say about the way in which local quarrels are encouraged by the big ones and merge with them; and this, of course, makes for bipolarization. As to whether there will eventually be two churches or many churches, there are other, balancing forces at work. In the short run, we can see a number of parties tending to exploit the split for their own purposes, balancing between the two giants, avoiding full commitment to either; and this makes for polycentrism. Even behind the iron curtain we can see this tendency, especially in the case of Rumania. On the other hand, to maintain ideological weight over a long period you need to have a state behind you. The Italian Communist Party, however brilliant some of its intellectuals may be, is a light-weight, because it does not have the money, it does not have the state apparatus and resources behind it, which in the long run can keep people in line. It is the powers like Russia, China or even Yugoslavia, with the people, the state resources and the continuity, which are likely to go on constituting the real nuclei, the decisive centres.

LABEDZ: The Italian Communist Party *has* got the money—it is in business in quite a big way.

DEVLIN: I wouldn't agree with Sherman, or perhaps I would agree only to a limited extent. State resources are important, of course. In fact, the big difference between factionalism today and the pre-war Trotskyist factionalism is that now the rebels can look to a major state with its resources of money and propaganda for aid and encouragement. But state resources aren't everything. I think Sherman picked a bad example in pointing to the Italian Communist Party. This is one instance of a party not having state power which still has very considerable influence in the world movement—not only in western Europe, especially Scandinavia, but also outside Europe. Many parties in the West are influenced by the Italian theories on structural reform, left-wing alliances and the parliamentary road to socialism; and many more are influenced by their insistence on the autonomy of each individual party and their slogan, 'Unity in diversity'.

SHERMAN: Yes, I should have described the Italian Party as a middle-weight rather than a light-weight. My point was that there are two heavy-weights—slugging it out now with little or no regard for the Queensberry rules. There are only two communist super-powers, each with major state resources, prestige and a claim to ideological leadership in the world movement. (The question of state power needs a lot of qualification anyhow—why, for instance, has Bulgaria remained a docile follower of the Moscow line while Rumania next door, with comparable state resources and the same satellite history, has been able to break away and defy Moscow to a degree which would have been inconceivable a few years ago?) But the point is that no foreign parties are going to look to Rumania for leadership and direction, though they may take a long, thoughtful look at its example. There may be sub-centres, but I think there will continue to be two main centres.

LABEDZ: So, in answer to my question, we have a combination of bipolarization and polycentrism. But which will dominate the mixture? Does this fragmentation that we are talking about point more to the crystallization of allegiances between Moscow and Peking, or does it tend to disintegrate the very idea of allegiance toward any centre, except perhaps some local or regional centre?

SHERMAN: I should put it another way. I should say that the conflict of allegiances tends in the long run to break down or erode the very allegiances which set it off. We can see this process at work in Latin America. Cuba counts for so much there; and the Cubans, particularly since 1961, have been working on the Latin American communist parties on their own account, as a communist third force. They have captured the Venezuelan Communist Party at one point; they have powerful influence in the Ecuadorean Party and in many other communist parties. Castro has been using the conflict between Moscow and Peking for his own purposes in this campaign. He deplores the split; he poses as being above it; and yet he profits from it. He comes forward with his specifically Latin-American example, and he tells young militants, in effect: 'Look—instead of fighting the imperialists, here you are fighting one another, because you are involved with these non-Latin-Americans. Forget about the Moscow Declaration, and listen to the Havana Declaration!'

DEVLIN: Well, Latin America as a whole is rather a special case, but it's a very important one. I agree with you that in Latin America Castroism has emerged as a virtual third force in the ideological free-for-all. The primary struggle in most countries is between the old-guard leadership—trained in the Comintern, habitually loyal to Moscow, and many of them now committed to the more-or-less parliamentary way to socialism—between them and Castroism in the broader sense of the word. Castroism goes beyond direct Cuban influence. Understood in this wider sense, it is revolutionary voluntarism with no very precise doctrinal basis to it, but still a political force which appeals to militants of very different kinds. We have seen in many Latin American countries how it attracts not only dissidents from the communist parties but Trotskyites and discontented left-wing militants from non-communist parties like APRA (American Revolutionary Popular Alliance) in Peru. The MIR (Movement of the Revolutionary Left) in Peru and the MOEC (Workers', Students' and Peasants' Movement) in Bolivia are not communist-controlled, but they are allies of Castroism; and, because they represent the revolutionary impulse, they also fit into the Chinese world strategy.

LABEDZ: On the other hand, we have also some evidence of a direct influence of the Sino-Soviet conflict on this Latin-American fragmentation. For more than two years now we have had two rival communist parties in Brazil, one pro-Soviet and the other pro-Chinese, which publishes a journal, *A Classe Operaria.** In January 1964 an explicitly pro-Chinese faction claimed to have taken over the Peruvian Communist Party at a national conference, but secretary-general Acosta still claims to lead the party for Moscow, and controls the party paper, *Unidad*—a pro-Chinese gang recently stormed and wrecked the office. There are other factions, too, which have specifically pledged loyalty to Peking.

DEVLIN: Yes; I should have gone on to say that, although in Latin America the struggle generally is one between Castroism and the old guard, still this struggle in each country will tend to become associated directly with the Sino-Soviet conflict, and will tend to find expression in Sino-Soviet terms. So, for example, when the Marxist Popular Vanguard emerges in Chile, it will send a manifesto to the Chinese Communist Party and will align itself specifically with Peking's positions. And, as you say, the same is true of other countries.

* After the overthrow of Goulart, the two Brazilian Communist Parties went underground. The pro-Chinese elements pointed out that the 'reformist' tactics of the secretary of the pro-Soviet Party, Luiz Carlos Prestes, facilitated the *coup*.

LABEDZ: This is where the Guelphs and Ghibellines come into the picture. And can this mechanism—this tendency for local struggles to become associated with the larger Sino-Soviet conflict—can it be detected not only in Latin America but in other parts of the world too?

SHERMAN: It certainly can. This was one of the points I had in mind when I spoke of the importance of state power, and said there would continue to be two main centres. Small factions can add a cubit or two to their stature by appealing to Peking. On the other hand, you have the other tendency, toward polycentrism and greater autonomy, which is itself in great measure a result of the Sino-Soviet dispute.

LABEDZ: Perhaps one can distinguish here between different phases, the short term and the long term. With the Sino-Soviet conflict dominating the whole world movement, the earlier stages of factionalism make it necessary for a party or faction to align itself with one side or the other. But in that very process it grows in autonomy, and the situation may develop into a more polycentric phase, with regional groupings, or even a tendency toward national communism.

DEVLIN: I think this is a very important point. The fact is that, although the anti-revisionist factions look to China, and get aid and encouragement from it, still these various factional struggles have, to a considerable extent, passed beyond the control of either Moscow or Peking and have developed a momentum of their own. Even if the Russians and Chinese managed somehow to patch up their differences —and at the moment this seems more unlikely than ever—this would not necessarily put an end to the process of fragmentation and ferment in the world movement.

SHERMAN: One sign of that is the present proliferation of factionalist publications. This is an expression of that momentum you talked about. These people are committed to a local fight, and they are hardly going to lay down their arms just because Mao Tse-tung whistles for a cease-fire—if he does—because in the last analysis he has no means of exercising direct control over them.

DEVLIN: These rebel publications also show that factionalism is becoming institutionalized, so to speak, and therefore more lasting. I looked into this recently and found that new pro-Chinese publications have been coming out at the rate of almost two a month, and they're distributed all over the world, from Australia to Argentina. In this recent period alone we have had *La Voix du Peuple* in

Belgium, *Die Rote Fahne* in Austria, *De Rode Vlag* in Holland, *L'Etincelle* in Switzerland, *Vanguard* in Britain, another *Vanguard* in Australia as well as *The Australian Communist*, one in Denmark called *Orientering*. Then there is *Revolution*, the magnificently-produced magazine which Jacques Vergès edits in Paris.* And, of course, these are added to existing factionalist publications—in France, for instance, there's quite an array of them.

SHERMAN: One came out a few months ago in Argentina—*El Obrero*.

DEVLIN: One should mention, too, that these publications are also found in clandestine communist movements. In December 1963 there appeared the first number of a rival version of the Spanish CP organ, *Mundo Obrero*, calling for the overthrow of the pro-Soviet leadership; and then in February (1964) we had the first number of *Proletario*, an anti-party monthly apparently produced by some pro-Chinese exiles.

LABEDZ: I'd like to take up Devlin's point that local factionalism tends to develop a momentum of its own, and explore it a little further. Now, one result of the general fragmentation is that communist parties are acquiring more local roots—they are having to present themselves as more independent, more in tune with local needs and interests. The question is whether this tendency will apply also to the pro-Chinese factions.

DEVLIN: I think so. In fact, one can already see this happening in some countries. In France, for instance, we have a number of factions which support the Chinese revolutionary line but criticize the Chinese for not having denounced and renounced Stalinism—the groups behind *La Voie Communiste* and *Le Communiste*. The *Ritorniamo a Lenin* group in Italy has taken a similar stand.†

SHERMAN: But this, surely, is what we might call a general trend, rather than a local deviation. This pro-revolution, anti-Stalin line is substantially that of the Trotskyites. Incidentally, we should perhaps say something about the Trotskyite attempt to climb on the Sinophile bandwagon in Latin America and western Europe.

LABEDZ: It's a complicated question, since the Trotskyites are also divided among themselves, in spite of the 'reunion congress' of the

* In 1965 *Revolution* ceased to appear.
† In the summer of 1964 a pro-Chinese group in Milan began publishing a new journal, *Nuova Unita*.

Fourth International held in the summer of 1963. There are several Trotskyite tendencies, each with its own centre: the 'United Secretariat', the 'International Committee', and the so-called 'Latin American Bureau'.

DEVLIN: On second thoughts, the *Voie Communiste* and *Ritorniamo a Lenin* factions represent more than a merely local deviation. But there are examples of local deviations, too. For instance, in Japan the revisionists led by Kasuga, who left the Japanese Communist Party or were expelled at the time of the Eighth Congress in 1961, split into two groups early in 1962 over the question of national strategy. Kasuga now leads the smaller of the two factions, and the two between them are producing three anti-party publications. This shows not only that factions are not immune to factionalism, but that factions, like parties, are affected by local conditions and the trend to polycentrism. The fact that the old Comintern system of 'transmission belts' has gone means inevitably that factions in each country will tend in time to develop along national lines, following their own path when it seems fit; because, after all, there is no prospect of a new International of the Comintern type emerging on either side of the great divide.

LABEDZ: Not a new Comintern, of course; yet the Chinese challenge to the Russians implies an attempt to form a new, if looser, International of anti-revisionist parties and factions. Their message is that they are going to replace Moscow in the leadership of the international movement, in the same way as Lenin replaced the old reformist social-democratic leadership; but this, surely, is nonsense.

SHERMAN: They should learn that history does not repeat itself, and that in the early 'sixties you cannot do what Lenin did in the early 'twenties. Differentiation along national or regional lines is here to stay, I think. This has some interesting results. In Latin America the effect of the Sino-Soviet conflict, combined with Castroism, has been to produce a greater emphasis on revolutionary violence. In western Europe it is having the opposite effect, with violence being played down or even renounced, and a lot of stress being placed instead on the 'peaceful way'. If this process goes on, in a few years' time we may be asking at what point does a communist party cease to be communist. In the capitalist countries, at least, the barriers which divide the communists from the rest of the left wing of the working-class movement may in the course of time become blurred.

LABEDZ: Surely the criterion here should be whether or not a party has abandoned, in theory or in practice, the Leninist formula. By that I mean a single party, or at least a coalition securely controlled by a single party, ruling in the name of the proletariat.

DEVLIN: One must remember here how much the communist world has changed since the death of Stalin. The Russians are now in a much more pragmatic mood, and are ready to accept quite a lot of doctrinal deviations in parties which were formerly required to toe the line laid down by Moscow. They have let the Italian Communist Party virtually abandon the doctrine of the dictatorship of the proletariat. Togliatti now calmly envisages the prospect that if his party comes to power, probably in alliance with other left-wing forces, it may be voted out of power again by the electors; and this means throwing the dictatorship of the proletariat on what the Chinese would call the rubbish-heap of history. Even the more dogmatic French Party, as a result of its efforts to woo the socialists, has come to admit that one can have a multi-party approach to socialism. The Russians are more pragmatic and tolerant because they are on the defensive, trying to keep their followers behind them even if it means letting them get out of step. The Chinese, being on the offensive, can stand by the letter of the past doctrine that the Russians and their allies have abandoned or modified.

SHERMAN: And the Soviets in return are trying to give a dogma a bad name and hang it!

LABEDZ: The question is whether the changes introduced by, say, the Italians are real changes, or whether they are merely verbal concessions to local conditions—that is, if the Italian Communist Party does come to power, will it really let itself be voted out again, or will it kick away the parliamentary ladder and establish the 'dictatorship of the proletariat'? Are the 'revisionists' not perhaps trying to preserve the essence while giving up the shadow? This, of course, nobody can answer, because it has, perhaps fortunately, not been put to the test yet.

DEVLIN: But I think the essence must be affected by the shadow, or lack of a shadow. When doctrine conflicts with reality, reality will win every time. The common feature here is opportunism; and one ought to note that it is not confined to the Soviet side of the ideological dispute. For instance, the Indonesian Communist Party is one of the foremost supporters of China's revolutionary world strategy, but in its domestic policy it is completely revisionist and opportunist, as the Italian communists gleefully pointed out in a *Rinascita* article in the summer of 1963. Chairman Aidit has even gone so far as to woo what he calls 'national capitalists'.

SHERMAN: Polycentrism again, on the Chinese side, or rather, at Chinese expense. The fact is that, although the Chinese can win supporters, they cannot impose a pattern. For one thing, as we have agreed, they have simply no means of exercising control, no organizational levers. In the second place, the Chinese revolutionary pattern just isn't applicable to many countries. As the Russians would say, rightly, the 'objective conditions' aren't there.

DEVLIN: There's an amusing example of that in Switzerland, where a tiny pro-Chinese Swiss Communist Party broke away in September 1963 from the pro-Soviet party, which is itself pretty insignificant.

SHERMAN: A flea upon a flea, in fact!

DEVLIN: Exactly. Well, these disciples of Mao held a national conference in November 1963 and adopted a programme which consisted entirely of demands for what the Italians would call structural reforms. It started with a demand for a ten per cent wage increase all round, and ended weakly with a call for 'libraries and other institutions'. There was no hint of violence, no plan for the transition period and the dictatorship of the proletariat. The fact is that bloody revolution just isn't a feasible proposition in Switzerland, and in quite a few other countries.

LABEDZ: The Swiss group may be made up of cranks, but that brings us on to an important point—the formation of secessionist, pro-Chinese communist parties in the recent period, and the implications this has for the Sino-Soviet dispute and for the world movement as a whole—if one can still speak of the world movement as a whole. How many of these secessionist parties are there at the moment?

DEVLIN: Well, there are Brazil, Peru, Belgium, Switzerland, Ceylon and Australia, the latest. It looks as if India will be next, or maybe Chile.

LABEDZ: There's also some doubt about Spain. The pro-Chinese faction—or one pro-Chinese faction—claims to have held a national conference somewhere in Spain in February 1964, at which they say they deposed the Carrillo leadership and appointed a new leadership of Marxist-Leninists, pending a national congress. But one doesn't really know what this means, if anything. It's very hard to find out just what is happening inside these clandestine parties.

SHERMAN: The Communist Party of Brazil was the first of these break-away parties. It split off from Prestes's Brazilian Communist Party early in 1962. That will deserve a place in the history books some day.

DEVLIN: Brazil is a special case. You remember the break-away Brazilian party's reply to the Soviet 'Open Letter' of 14 July: the Brazilians got very annoyed over the Soviet claim that the Chinese were responsible for the Brazilian split. They said the split was due to internal causes—their rebellion against Prestes's revisionist line—and that at the time they didn't even know the Chinese arguments. Well, that's a bit too ingenuous, of course, but I think there's something in it. I think the Brazilian split *was* primarily the result of an internal struggle for power. As far as I know, the Chinese didn't start publicizing the Brazilian split until last August or September (1963). The other secessionist parties are different. For one thing, they came considerably later. For another, in all of them—except perhaps Switzerland—we have evidence of direct Chinese intervention and support. This is a deliberate splitting campaign, not just a matter of encouraging pro-Chinese factions within the parties.

LABEDZ: If there is such a splitting campaign—and I agree with you, and with the Russians, that it looks that way now—the doctrinal justification for it was provided in Chou Yang's famous lecture, published on 26 December 1963, which was taken up and elaborated in the *People's Daily/Red Flag* article of 4 February 1964. The argument is that splits are, in fact, inevitable and to be welcomed. Revisionism was bound to arise, and now it is bound to be swept aside by so-called Marxist-Leninists who stand by the revolutionary gospel.

SHERMAN: A new slogan—'Workers of the world, disunite: you have nothing to lose but your revisionists!' Of course, they are only carrying the old fallacy a stage further. Why should the inevitable dialectic of the splitting process stop with them? Indeed, why should it stop anywhere?

LABEDZ: There is one further point that ought to be made about these secessionist parties: it will now be much more difficult, if not impossible, to settle things by hammering out a compromise at an all-party conference, as in 1960. I don't see how they could agree now on who should be invited. I cannot see either side abandoning *their* communist party—the Russians couldn't, and the Chinese wouldn't.

DEVLIN: I agree. But I don't think there's much chance of a genuine conference anyhow—I mean a genuine all-party attempt to settle differences through compromises. The Chinese have gone so far along the road of world-wide factionalism, and have been so successful, that they can hardly pull back now and lose face. Besides, as we saw at the time of the trial balloons in September and October 1963, the Russians would have some trouble in rounding up the officially pro-Soviet parties for anything like an excommunication conference. A lot of parties have gained more independence and freedom of manœuvre because of the dispute, and it would suit them to have things go on as they are, with neither a showdown nor a reconciliation.

SHERMAN: This would depend to some extent on how much internal factionalism they had to contend with, and how much of a real threat it was.

LABEDZ: Although the process has acquired its own momentum, neither the actors, nor the observers may yet realize its extent. This may account for some of the Soviet tactical failures. After Khrushchev's Budapest visit in April 1964, it became clear that his renewed attempts to excommunicate the Chinese communists at an international conference had again failed, and, as a result, the Soviet resumption of polemics with the Chinese in the press came with a whimper rather than with a bang. It is no less acrimonious for that and will further encourage internal and international factionalism.

How does this fragmentation of the formerly unitary world communist movement affect the front organizations? These are the classical instruments which were very important in acquiring influence, if not control, over the mass movements in non-communist countries. In fact, in western Europe since the war the communist parties have had very little direct influence over the masses, except in France and Italy. The question is how the Sino-Soviet dispute has affected these transmission belts, because without them many communist parties will simply lose their local political significance altogether.

DEVLIN: I think the Sino-Soviet split has largely ruined these transmission belts so far as their effective use in western countries is concerned.

SHERMAN: It has changed them from front organizations into battle-front organizations.

DEVLIN: Exactly. They were, in fact, fated to become battle-grounds once the Chinese had embarked on their challenge to Soviet leadership of the world movement. They started this factionalist struggle in earnest in 1960. The Peking session of the General Council of the World Federation of Trade Unions in June 1960 was one of the first known occasions on which the Chinese lobbied delegates both communist and non-communist, and earned for themselves a stinging letter from the Central Committee of the French Communist Party. From that time onwards we have seen the same struggle, growing more intense all the time, at every meeting of every front organization that we know about—the World Federation of Trade Unions, the International Organization of Journalists, the World Federation of Democratic Youth, and so forth.

The Soviet side had a big advantage in this struggle, because these international front organizations had been set up under Stalin, and their secretariats were staffed largely by east and west European communists, their headquarters were in eastern or western Europe, and the Russians have been able throughout to keep the upper hand organizationally, in terms of delegate strength. The Chinese have not given up the struggle on that account, but have waged it more and more bitterly, and have brought it out into the open; and they have tried a very shrewd riposte of their own by moving to set up separate Afro-Asian organizations—for trades unions, students, scientists and journalists—which they can dominate, and which will be open rivals to the original, Soviet-dominated front organizations.

LABEDZ: I agree that in Europe the front organizations have largely come to the end of their influence, because to a great extent they have been exposed as communist-manipulated instruments, and once the communists began to fight among themselves, that manipulation could be hidden no longer. In the underdeveloped countries, however, we have a different problem. The struggle there has had its ups and downs. For instance, the Russians suffered a defeat at the meeting of the Afro-Asian Peoples' Solidarity Organization at Moshi, Tanganyika, in February 1963, because of the rather clever racialist tactics of the Chinese; but this was largely reversed at the Nicosia meeting of the Afro-Asian Peoples' Solidarity Organization executive in September. The next meeting, in Algiers, witnessed an even more ferocious ideological struggle, but the net result may be one envisaged neither by the Soviet nor the Chinese communists, since some of the African delegates were clearly bored and annoyed by this feud.

At the moment it seems that, parallel to these divisions in the old-established front organizations, another process has set in, which Devlin has already mentioned, and that is the creation of rival regional organizations by the Chinese. I wonder how the establishment of such parallel organizations would affect the influence of the Russians and Chinese respectively in, say, Africa, and how it would indirectly affect the development of Afro-communism?

SHERMAN: It's a bit early to talk of Afro-communism, isn't it? At the moment Africans are all so busy being black that they haven't time to be red. Anyhow, I think that in order to understand this question one has to realize that a basic change in the character of front organizations, or some of them, took place even before the Sino-Soviet split. It began with the change in Soviet strategy towards the *tiers monde* after Stalin's death and following the emergence of nationalist, revolutionary, and authoritarian régimes in Afro-Asia, like Nasser's in Egypt, Soekarno's in Indonesia, Nkrumah's in Ghana, Sekou Touré's in Guinea, and so on. The old-fashioned front organizations thrived on European innocents who could be drawn in and easily exploited by the communists. But it was not so easy to dominate and exploit nationalist revolutionaries like Nasser and Nkrumah, because they were in a similar business themselves. From the first they refused to have much to do with the old-established fronts; they had no desire to support or be committed by organizations in which they did not have their share of control. So the Afro-Asian People's Solidarity Organization was set up in Cairo, with the Russians, the Chinese, the Egyptians, the Indonesians and others all taking a considerable share in it, and all trying to use it for their own purposes. You had what you might call a pluralistic front there, not a monolithic organization. The dominant force in Africa today is nationalism, combined with 'Africanism', and it won't be so easy for the Russians or the Chinese to corral Africans through front organizations. The fronts are more like emporia for horse-trading and mutual back-scratching—part cooperation and part competition in militancy.

LABEDZ: And how, in turn, does this struggle within the front organizations—either Afro-Asian or international—influence the central Sino-Soviet conflict?

SHERMAN: The effect can only be to make it more intense, surely. If it had not been for these front organizations the differences between the Chinese and the Russians could have been kept beneath the surface longer; they could have worked on them with what you might call ideological secret diplomacy. But the Chinese were led to take the offensive in the front organizations because they were dominated by the Russians and because the Chinese, not being in the United Nations and having far fewer diplomatic links with other countries, needed these organizations much more than the Russians did. But when the Chinese attacked, the Russians simply were left with no alternative but to fight back, and they became more and more embroiled. So here we have again to some extent a self-perpetuating process which cannot be stopped merely by Moscow and Peking agreeing to stop open polemics. For instance, if you have an Afro-Asian solidarity meeting in Nicosia, and the test-ban agreement is on the agenda, then you have to debate it; and that means trouble.

LABEDZ: Now, if we can come back to our starting-point, which is the question of the general fragmentation within the communist movement itself—how will this process of confused and shifting allegiances influence the rival Russian and Chinese claims for world leadership? It seems to me doubtful if the emergence of pro-Chinese factions or even parties in different countries and the struggle to control the front organizations will do much more than end the isolation of the Chinese. It will not mean that the Chinese will some day have the kind of ascendancy in the world movement, or even a section of the world movement, that Moscow once had.

DEVLIN: I think it is clear that neither side can have leadership in the way that we knew it in the past under Stalin. The fact is that with Stalin's death—and even earlier, with the end of 'socialism in one country'—it became inevitable that the various parties, non-ruling as well as ruling parties, should acquire more independence. The habit of solidarity is still strong, and the doctrinal impulse toward unity is still there; but more and more parties are now recognizing that they have this greater independence, and are beginning to exercise it. The Sino-Soviet factionalist conflict has accelerated this process. Neither the individual parties nor the anti-party factions can be treated any longer as docile followers: they are allies, sometimes reluctant allies, who have to be courted.

There are plenty of examples of this. In October 1963 we had the Italian Communist Party standing up and rejecting the clear, if implicit, Soviet call for a conference of all parties. We have seen the little Norwegian Party, which is completely insignificant in its own country and which lies in the geopolitical shadow of the Soviet Party, declaring that it is going to try to keep out of the Sino-Soviet struggle altogether. And after the resumption of Sino-Soviet polemics in April 1964, the Rumanian Party made a statement which, in effect, came as close to a declaration of neutrality in the Sino-Soviet dispute as one can expect to get in the east European context. This kind of thing would have been inconceivable even a few years ago.

LABEDZ: This is the tendency toward national or regional communism about which I spoke at the beginning, and which is itself one aspect of the general loosening of bonds in the world movement. The process of disintegration which began in 1948 with the condemnation of Yugoslavia is now in full flood, with a confused and confusing struggle going on between the parties, inside the parties, outside the parties and in the front organizations. The picture is, in fact, a good deal more complicated than we have been able to indicate. For instance, we have made only a passing reference to the involvement of the Trotskyites. We have said nothing of the existence of factional patterns, in western Europe, and elsewhere, which pre-date the Sino-Soviet dispute—the revisionist rebellions in Denmark and Holland, for example, or the Stalinist secession in Sweden.

At this stage it is difficult if not impossible to predict the consequences for individual parties and factions, as well as for the world movement. However, one general conclusion seems obvious: the old picture of the international communist movement does not fit reality any longer; and if one does not take this basic fact into account, one cannot hope to understand the present world situation.

8

The Uncommitted Communist Parties

SPEAKERS

Gordon Barrass

Richard Rockingham Gill

Leopold Labedz

8. The Uncommitted Communist Parties

LABEDZ: At various times and in various countries we have seen communists stoutly denying the existence of any quarrel in their ranks, or wringing their hands over the folly and pity of it all, or boldly announcing their own proposals for reconciling the protagonists. The attempts to 'paper over the cracks' go back, indeed, as far as the appearance of the cracks themselves. You remember the Bucharest meeting in the summer of 1960, when the Albanians first aligned themselves with the Chinese, and the Russians, having failed to isolate the Chinese by a surprise attack, agreed to a world communist conference. And this conference, the conference of the Eighty-one Parties, took place in October and November of the same year, ending in the celebrated Statement which was a mere formal compromise, a 'mechanical amalgamation' of formulae from both sides. Neither the Russians nor the Chinese changed their views or their tactics and the compromise broke down visibly at the 22nd Congress.

But let us focus our memories for a moment on the 1960 meeting of the Eighty-one Parties. It was when he was on his way to this Moscow parley that Aidit, the leader of the Indonesian Communist Party, revealed in an interview he gave to the Polish paper *Trybuna Ludu* that he was seeking a compromise formula to which the Chinese, the Russians and everybody could give their assent. And he played in fact a considerable part, it seems, in finding it; at any rate the Indonesian Party claimed credit for this afterwards. What were Aidit's motives, and how typical were they for the motives of other communist leaders who, in the intervening years, have from time to time sought to pour oil on the troubled Sino-Soviet waters?

GILL: There is surely no single type here. I am reminded of the story of the Irishman who, asked by an American during the last World War if it were true that his country was neutral, replied with a heavy Irish wink: 'It is indeed, sir! Neutral against Germany.' And in the line-up of communist parties over the Sino-Soviet dispute we could label the Indonesians and the Japanese, say, as 'neutral against Moscow', or 'uncommitted against the Russians', in the same sense as we could call Castro 'neutral against China'.

Aidit's motives for non-commitment, to start with him, have, as far as I can see, astonishingly little to do with ideology; they seem almost entirely opportunist and nationalist. He is the leader of the most powerful non-ruling communist party in Asia, a party with a very strong foothold in the system of government and with perpetual hopes of being given a foothold by Soekarno in the cabinet itself. He knows perfectly well that Indonesia benefits from enormous doses of aid—military and to some extent economic—from the Soviet Union. So that despite his leaning toward Peking on ideological grounds—he is all for more and better revolutionary wars and damns Malaysia as 'imperialist'—and despite, perhaps, an ethnic affinity with the Chinese as fellow-Asians, he knows just as well as his non-committed brother Castro that his only hope of adequate material support is in the Moscow camp. After all, Indonesia is a country of some ninety million souls and, as an Indonesian, Aidit is interested in the roubles and the guns that only the Russians can furnish in significant quantities. Hence, I think, his desperate initial efforts to 'paper over the cracks', though the failure of those efforts, and perhaps the willingness of Peking, unlike Moscow, to give verbal backing at least to his Borneo campaign, seem to have led him into a progressively more Pekinese stance over the last few years.

BARRASS: Another consideration that should help to keep Aidit in a neutral position is surely the association of China in Indonesian minds with the rather unpopular Chinese minority in their own country. Maoism certainly has a lot to offer to Aidit; but if he were to voice this too loudly, he would have to reckon with more of those unpleasant anti-Chinese demonstrations that took place, for example, in Jakarta during Liu-Shao Chi's visit. And after all it is not so many years since Soekarno's régime was proposing to push the entire Chinese community out of the country, and many harsh words were bandied about between Peking and Jakarta.

GILL: I quite agree that Aidit must take this factor too into his calculations—and yet this is again a factor having everything to do with nationalism and nothing with ideology. But it is a measure of Aidit's latter-day bias toward the Chinese position that his press still adopts the Peking equation: modern revisionists—i.e. Khrushchev and Tito —equal United States lackeys. Whereas the North Vietnamese Party, of course, has not hit upon this interesting identification and does not hold that those modern revisionists are necessarily United States lackeys!

But to return to the Indonesian Party and its progress towards

China: there is a whole series of symptoms, but they still do not add up to total commitment. In 1959 Aidit rejected the people's communes as a model for Indonesia, but also dissociated himself from Khrushchev's attack on Stalin. He refused to support Soviet criticisms of Albania—knowing they were aimed at China—but in February 1963 demonstrated his fence-sitting position by calling for an end to '*all* mutual accusations' among the parties. Aidit has joined Mao in condemning Tito, and taken China's side against India, and against the test-ban. Yet during the anti-Chinese riots of May 1963 he sided wholly with his non-communist President, Soekarno—for purely opportunist, nationalist reasons.

LABEDZ: A moment ago you were contrasting the Indonesian Party, 'neutral against Moscow', with Castro whom you call 'neutral against Peking'. But of course one of the differential factors here is simply that Castro's party is in power and Aidit's isn't. Castro, in other words, has to sit on two stools for reasons of economic dependence, whereas Aidit can afford to lean more heavily toward Peking since he is still concerned with gaining power; economic dependence is Soekarno's headache, not his; that has yet to come!

GILL: True, but in order to achieve power within the Indonesian cabinet, power that seems so nearly in his grasp, Aidit cannot afford to prejudice his own potential chances, or Soekarno's actual chances, of large-scale Soviet aid. If he did that, or appeared to be doing that, Soekarno would be still less inclined to give him that coveted foothold in the cabinet.

LABEDZ: You mentioned another non-ruling party in the same part of the world that you consider to be 'neutral against Moscow'—the Japanese.

GILL: Yes. The majority of this party, and of its periodicals, are in pro-Chinese hands, and it has now openly broken its ties with Moscow. In August 1963 a Japanese communist delegation was received in the Kremlin by Brezhnev, and more recently a Secretary of the Japanese Party went to Moscow on a mission that looked a little like the Rumanian visit to Peking. Up to a certain point these ambivalent tactics were obviously not unconnected with the fact that the Japanese Party's money used to come from both Soviet and Chinese sources, and though of the two the Chinese paid better, the Party treasurers were no doubt loth to forgo the funds flowing from the more distant patron. On the other hand, when a number of pro-Soviet leaders were purged from the Japanese Party, Moscow continued to publish *Problems of Peace and Socialism* in Japanese for the benefit of the remaining Khrushchevite communists inside—and now outside! —the Japanese Party.

LABEDZ: Now that we have mentioned the role played by geography and cash, and other such un-ideological factors in determining an individual party's stance, perhaps we can afford to move back for a moment to more general and theoretical fields—to the basic idea of non-commitment, in fact. Before the war we were familiar with the idea of neutrality exemplified, say, by Sweden or Switzerland. This was a legal concept designed to protect the neutral state from the effects of war; it had nothing to do with that state's sympathies, which were sometimes quite clearly on one side or the other in the dispute from which it had politically dissociated itself. It was only after the last war that we heard of 'neutralism', a quite different, political attitude, the attitude primarily of emergent countries first in Asia and then in Africa who saw the Cold War as irrelevant to their values and hostile to their interests. And now there has been a further move, from the concept of neutralism, with its overtones of moral indifference which began to seem cowardly or reactionary to some of the third world leaders, onward to the new notion of 'non-alignment'. 'Non-alignment' is a formula favoured by countries which are unwilling to commit themselves, politically or militarily, to either bloc, but at the same time are reluctant to imply that they equally reject the ideologies of both. The Chinese are in fact exploiting this hesitation now by arguing—as Chou En-lai did in Mogadishu at the end of his African trip—that you can be ideologically on the side of the socialist states against imperialism and still stay non-aligned!

Now the question I want to put is whether all or any of these concepts—neutrality, neutralism, non-alignment—make sense *inside* the communist camp, as defining an attitude toward the Sino-Soviet quarrel itself? After all, the communist movement is based on a black-and-white view of history that divides humanity into the children of light and the children of darkness. And you cannot really have a neutral position between light and darkness. Or, as communist terminology has it, you cannot have a third side to the barricades. Can there be a third side to those barricades that Marx and Lenin never foresaw—the ones between China and Russia?

It is true that the immediate political motives for a given party's pro-Soviet or pro-Chinese tactics may be concerned with economic or military aid, with rivalry between real and potential leaders and so forth. But if we look at this matter in a longer perspective, and consider how far the communist mentality is conditioned by doctrines that exclude the middle and leave no room for compromises, then can we expect that any of these parties which are so frantically trying to stay on the fence can hope to preserve their perches indefinitely?

BARRASS: Yes, I think some of them will be able to do just that for a very long time. I would apply this especially to some of the European parties that are more or less non-aligned—the Norwegians, the British Party, the Italians, in a different sense the Poles, and now again the Yugoslavs who, however far the Chinese drive them into the Russians' arms, are ready to jump out of that embrace again whenever there is any suggestion of a revival of Cominform. The Yugoslavs are keen on pointing out that there is no theoretical justification in Marxism for any 'centre' to the communist world at all. They are all 'children of light'—but the light comes from different places, and each child must look up and see the light and then decide what it should do, in its own situation, in terms of what it sees. No one outside a country, say the Yugoslavs very pointedly, can understand that country's problems or give good advice. So the communist conversation these days has to be a multilateral one.

It was of course the Russian idea that the international communist movement should only have one centre, and that this lent a special unity to Marxism-Leninism; and perhaps the Chinese shared this view when they thought they could take over the leadership of the movement without any phase of disruption; but the parties of Europe, especially western Europe, seem to be challenging this assumption radically.

LABEDZ: If this picture is true—this picture of polycentrism snow-balling, of a final abandonment of the unitary character of the communist movement—can we expect these non-aligned parties to go a step further: not merely to stay sitting on two stools but to try and erect fresh stools of their own design, fashioned to suit their own special anatomies?

GILL: Oh, I am sure this process is taking place before our very eyes. The Italian Party, I am convinced, is trying to set up just such a new stool, not only for itself, but for the whole of western Europe, on which, however, it will itself occupy the most central and commanding position. Again, I should say that Castro and the Cuban Party have for a long time shown signs of wanting to establish a neutralist niche for Latin America. Castro, after all, has refused to approve one of Khrushchev's major initiatives of 1963; he has refused to sign the test-ban treaty. Yet he regularly goes to Moscow and makes pro-Khrushchev statements there, and comes back with contracts for the sale of Cuban sugar at what appear to be very inflated prices.

In a third region of the world, Asia, Aidit appears to be bidding for some kind of ideological leadership for Indonesia, and I think in the long run he might stand some chance of success. And in the very long run we may see a 'third road' trend—or will it be a sixth or seventh by then?—in Africa too; so far, of course, there are not enough communists in that continent to support one.

Many of the suggestions made by the various parties for overcoming the present split in the world movement have been predicated, incidentally, on bilateral talks between the two parties immediately concerned, or between a larger number of parties, but then on a bilateral basis at first, with regional conferences later. Now, if such regional conferences are held—and possibly some already have been—I think we may see bids by, for example, the Italian Party to take over the leadership in western Europe from parties which it regards as retrograde, like the French.

BARRASS: Yes, I think the Norwegian Party furnishes an interesting example of this. At the end of 1962 and the beginning of 1963, for instance, the old party chairman Lovlien went to Peking to try and mediate in the dispute; troubled with revisionism in his own party, he no doubt hoped something could be done to quieten down the big argument that feeds the little ones. He came back from Peking, but the rift was not noticeably affected. Then during 1963 he was succeeded as chairman by Jørgen Vogt, who went to Moscow in October, where the Russians tried to persuade him to take up a pro-Russian stand. He did not like this. He went back to Norway and, just as he returned, the Italians sent a message saying that the time had come for new relations between the parties, that relations must be based on equality between them, and that there was now a need for meetings of the west European communist parties.

LABEDZ: ... and no need for international party meetings about the Sino-Soviet rift. The Italian case points to a curious discrepancy between ideological commitment and practical political non-commitment. Ideologically there is no doubt that the Italian party is on the right of the spectrum and is very firmly committed against the Chinese line. Yet at the same time the Italians are equally firmly committed against that international conference which the Russians are trying to press upon the other parties and which has been repeatedly postponed. In our attempt to classify the reactions of various parties to the Sino-

Soviet rift, then, it seems pointless to fasten on any one criterion, since the political behaviour of each party is the result of a mixture of motives, in which doctrine may point one way and tactical needs another. Instead of single symptoms we shall have to look out, as it were, for syndromes—associated groups of symptoms.

Yugoslavia, for example, represents an even more extreme case than Italy of a division between ideological commitment and political reluctance. The Yugoslav Party is one which has been made the butt of the Chinese attack—and was in fact the scapegoat *par excellence* at the time when Khrushchev could not be called a 'revisionist' but Tito palpably could—and yet this party has refused to commit itself to any project for an international communist conference which would pronounce a final anathema against the Chinese.

BARRASS: But Tito's reluctance has presumably different motivations from those of Togliatti's. To recall your own distinction, Togliatti is not in power; he has to take into account electoral considerations, the coherence of the party, the leadership situation, the adjustment to Italian democratic conditions and to the whole political and social situation there. But Tito *is* in power and has none of these problems— what are the reasons for *his* hesitation, then?

GILL: I think they are purely tactical. I do not believe for a moment that the Yugoslavs are really uncommitted, or neutralist, or non-aligned—that they really *want* to be any of these things. I am sure they are militantly anti-Peking in their hearts.

However, the Yugoslavs seem to think it desirable that some other party, preferably the Soviet Party itself, should take upon itself the onus of calling for the international conference that would excommunicate the Chinese—and this largely, I am sure, for the very reason that the Yugoslavs were one of the original causes of the rift, the first post-war heretics, the seed-bed of revisionism. Another tactical consideration in Tito's mind, I suggest, is that in the event of a regional European communist grouping being formed, he may not want to be cut off from it. So, for the present, he joins Togliatti in opposing the idea of an immediate, worldwide conference. For anyone who took the opposite line would be sure to forfeit the support of several west European parties that are anxious for their own, practical purposes to stop the great rift from going too far too fast. The Norwegians, for example ...

BARRASS: Yes, it is strange how these aspirations to play a big role as an honest broker well up particularly among communist parties that are too small and debilitated to play any role at all in their own countries. The Norwegian Party, after all, has been dwindling fast since the end of the war; it has no deputies in parliament, and only three thousand members—for which it compensates by having three wings: pro-Chinese, pro-Russian, and 'national communist'.

And you find the same ambitions in that other weakling party, the British. You remember secretary Gollan's visit to Peking in 1962 and the subsequent resolution which, though it tried very hard to avoid condemning the Chinese, was still a Moscow-line statement. Well, none of these efforts at reconciliation has led to anything; the split merely deepened further.

LABEDZ: Quite—and no doubt similar conclusions are evolving in the minds of all the would-be honest brokers. But let us consider now, not the historic roots or even the present motives for 'communist non-commitment', but its possible effects in the future.

GILL: I think the Rumanian case is particularly instructive here. Just consider the probable effect of Maurer's unprecedented trip to Peking, with its unprecedented routing straight from Bucharest to Omsk, omitting Moscow altogether—a remarkable piece of touristic deviationism! The Rumanians may or may not agree with the Russians on the principles of their dispute with China, yet they made this anti-Soviet demonstration, and in April 1964 the party washed its hands of the dispute in a formal statement. So one result has been to strengthen the position of the party among Rumanian nationalists, who may say 'Here are the communists at last standing up to the Soviet Union!' Of course, these nationalists would not want a genuine reconciliation with the Chinese, but then they would appreciate that that was not really in Gheorghiu Dej's or Maurer's mind, just as we do.

A second result of the Rumanian tactics may be to encourage other east European parties to think: 'If the Rumanians can take this kind of independent initiative, so can we.' There may easily be a political backwash of this kind, inciting even those parties hitherto loyal to Khrushchev to wonder whether the correct policy henceforth will not be to outdo the Rumanians rather than leave the running to them. Hungary (where internal revisionism has gone farthest) is already making serious efforts to increase her economic cooperation with Austria. This is a step away from full reliance on Comecon towards closer cooperation with a country which is a member of one of the two Western economic communities, EFTA.

LABEDZ: What other east European leaders might emulate the Rumanian initiative?

BARRASS: Apart from the Hungarians, I should think Gomulka the most likely candidate. He has been lying low for some months, and if Khrushchev consulted him in January and in April 1964, I should think it was because he thought Gomulka might be tempted by some of the ideas now spawning among west European communists. And since then Khrushchev seems to have tried hard to keep the Rumanians isolated.

LABEDZ: Isolated, that is, among the east European group. Of course we have here to distinguish between short and long-term effects. Supposing, for example, that this tendency toward communist groupings leads to a condemnation of the Chinese, not by a world-wide conference but just by some European parties with Russian participation. Now will this smooth the path of any east European 'national communist' leader anxious to take independent initiatives? In the long run it will not hinder him, perhaps; but in the short run it could make his task harder. And that must apply to Gomulka.

In Budapest (in April 1964) Khrushchev hinted at some new organizational forms of cooperation between the east European communist régimes. He did not specify what he had in mind, but it was said in the context of the Sino-Soviet dispute.

Now let us turn our attention to a figure at the opposite end of the scale of 'non-aligned communists'—to Castro, with his devious game played between the Russians and the Chinese.

What is the immediate political relevance of Castro's refusal to commit himself? One which Gill mentioned was the symbolic effect of his refusal to sign the test-ban treaty. Well, this counted in 1963 but I am afraid that it will be forgotten during 1964, and forgotten still more as more time passes. On the real political level, we have oddities like Castro's 'Zanzibar House' in Havana, his sponsoring of broadcasts to America by the Negro publicist Robert Williams who has made frequent trips to Peking, and so on. These are Castro's sideshows of revolutionary activity and promotion of the Chinese line. But his situation is very different from that of the east European régimes with their state commitments; Castro allows himself a quite different margin of manœuvre.

GILL: And one must always remember, I think, that Castro's party is not really united behind him. At the very moment when he was negotiating with Khrushchev for his long-term sugar market in

Moscow, Peking chose to publish the works of Ché Guevara on guerrilla warfare, works that read remarkably like Mao Tse-tung's own writings in the fourth volume of his collected works. I cannot help thinking this was a gentle Chinese hint that Ché Guevara thinks in more Chinese terms than Castro does.

So I think it quite possible that the Cuban Party, in its particular circumstances, may choose to remain non-aligned even when most of the world's communist parties are obliged to stand up and be counted. Incidentally, one should not forget that the Soviet Party itself claimed, in *Kommunist*, only sixty-five of the world's parties as its supporters on the big issue. And subsequently, Suslov, in his report on the dispute to the Central Committee dropped even that figure.

LABEDZ: Well, we have considered a large array of particular parties suffering from all kinds of centrifugal and divisive tendencies, internal and external: perhaps we can make another attempt to generalize. Two kinds of reaction, broadly speaking, seem possible for the parties in this phase of growing polycentrism—or, to use a word sanctified by Soviet usage—of growing 'localism', the phenomenon that the textbooks warn against. One kind of reaction would be to accept increasingly the immediate choice forced upon the party in question by the various pressures emanating from Moscow and Peking, forced upon it by its dependence, economic, political, or military. And the other reaction would be to play the game of regional groupings in which the tendency would be to avoid commitment, and to avoid deepening the split which demands commitment.

Barrass has suggested that the west European parties, to take one region, will follow the second path of increasing non-commitment and evasion. Can this be said to cover the whole world movement, ruling and non-ruling parties alike? Or is it a tendency peculiar to western Europe, where the parties exist in a situation of relative affluence due to a high degree of industrialization?

BARRASS: I think the same tendency will prevail in eastern Europe too. As we have said, the Rumanian initiative is bound to have an effect on the other ruling parties round about. These parties are next to Russia and have the closest possible economic and political links with Russia, yet there is still nothing to prevent them from withholding their consent to any move for collective denunciation of the Chinese. And an anathema is considerably stultified when there is even one absentee from the service. As time goes on, I believe Khrushchev will be forced to consult with these nearby parties more and more, and that an east European bloc might emerge with certain common interests—

though I am far from certain what Russia's exact position *vis-à-vis* such a bloc would be.

LABEDZ: Peaceful coexistence between East and West, Khrushchev has cheerily assured us, will mean not less but more of a struggle on the ideological plane. What about peaceful coexistence, so to speak, between the two intra-communist camps in the Sino-Soviet schism? The non-aligned parties, at least, can hardly engage in a sharpening ideological struggle between the two giants. One might expect, on the contrary, that they would tend to play down ideological disagreements as part of their policy of disengagement. Yet what *raison d'être* does the communist movement retain in countries where it does not rule, once it sheds its ideological panoply?

GILL: Well, there is more than one kind of ideology available, and the common ideological element among all these parties that have stayed uncommitted is the ideology of their respective nationalisms. There may be questions of economic aid, too; there may be some drastic weakness and internal division such as afflicts the Norwegians; there may be some balance of calculations as in Vietnam, where Ho Chi Minh wants to avoid total submission to the Chinese yet realizes that Khrushchev is awfully far away. But in all these separate cases the major factor, often overlapping with those quoted, is that of nationalism.

One of the most interesting facets of the Rumanian case, for example, is the de-Russification that has gone on there, and which may be increasingly important in the future. The fact, for example, that the Maxim Gorky Institute has been given a new and Rumanian title. Or that the Rumanian edition of Moscow's propaganda weekly *New Times* has been closed down and replaced by a Rumanian version with a Rumanian name.

This sort of thing happened long ago in Yugoslavia; it has happened in Albania; it may yet spread to other parties—and not only to east European ones.

BARRASS: There is also the example of North Korea whose historians, as you know, have attacked the Russian Academy of Science for its *World History*, saying that it contains 'gross distortions' of the Korean past.

LABEDZ: If we may come back to western Europe for a moment: it is a curious fact that the parties which now seem to take radical ideology most seriously are in several cases left-socialist groups and not the official communist parties. This applies to the new Socialist Party of Proletarian Unity in Italy, to Larsen's party in Denmark, to the Socialist People's Party in Norway. Yet for all their doctrinal fervour, these parties have been conspicuously reluctant to commit themselves too explicitly on the Sino-Soviet issue. So this would appear to contradict your canon that non-alignment goes hand-in-hand with ideological apathy.

GILL: True, but what I suggested was that non-alignment will contribute among communist parties to the erosion of ideological interest; I cannot allow you to make me say, now, that non-alignment among these left-socialist parties, who have adopted neutralism for different reasons, will lead to the same result! Let's take a closer look at this 'erosion'. One factor in the ideological decay of the west European communist parties has been the need to attract votes in order to implement that programme of peaceful transition which Khrushchev has himself set up as the aim for all the west European parties. Another has been the general trend of Khrushchev's own thinking toward an extreme form of revisionism. It is hardly surprising that many communist parties in this region now seem to have a platform to the right of the left-socialist parties, considering that Khrushchev's own platform is so largely non-ideological, 'pragmatic' and opportunist. (He is forever justifying his latest theories by obscure paragraphs from the Marxist classics, or even by downright invention, it seems—as in the case of the famous 'Lenin letter' which Moscow found in five separate shorthand notebooks of the master's, unreadable to anybody in the world except for one Russian stenographer!)

Inevitably, then, the left-socialists are often made to seem, and probably are, better ideologists and better Marxists than the revisionist communists tied to Khrushchev's dubious coat-tails. But superior debating skill is not going to bring them to power, and I see every reason to expect that the creeping death of ideology will continue both among the European parties which remain faithful to Moscow—a strong majority, after all—and among the non-aligned communists.

LABEDZ: Every Marxist can find a quotation to suit himself in Lenin's works; and when he cannot, he says simply that 'Marxism is not a dogma but a guide to action'!

GILL: About as helpful a guide to action as the sibylline prophecies. And perhaps it is a striking sign of the times that the Rumanians have not yet thought it necessary to found any ideology at all in justification of their special road—even though they have a long land frontier with the U S S R, something Tito did not have to reckon with. It is not in ideology but in trade, economics, cultural affairs and foreign policy that the Rumanians are striking out on their own. Evidently Bucharest has decided that Moscow no longer dares to use her military might to ensure obedience, and therefore the 'uncommitted' road is wide open.

LABEDZ: And one wonders how long it will be before the remaining pro-Khrushchev parties realize the boon which the freedom of manœuvre brings.

9

Membership Trends and
Electoral Fortunes

SPEAKERS

Leonard Schapiro

R. V. Burks

Leopold Labedz

9. Membership Trends and Electoral Fortunes

LABEDZ: The question I should like us to discuss today is the impact of the Sino-Soviet dispute on the strength of the various communist parties outside the two communist blocs.

The word 'strength', of course, covers a multitude of sins. Some signs of strength can be measured mathematically—by the number of people who belong to the party, the number who vote for it and so on. Other kinds of strength can only be estimated by using one's political judgment. Again, there is the distinction between direct and indirect strength: communist parties have made a special art of the technique of influencing populations through various front organizations. We must examine all these ways of exerting strength and influence.

'The impact of the dispute on the strength of the parties,' we said. The word 'impact', too, has to be looked at closely. There is the impact on the party members, especially on the élite; and there is the impact on people who usually vote for the party or might be persuaded to—or not. You would expect the party members, the zealots, to be discouraged by the Sino-Soviet dispute, to lose their faith perhaps in two crucial points of Marxist-Leninist belief—the legitimacy of the party's mission and the inevitability of the historical process.

But how does the Sino-Soviet dispute affect the mass of mere sympathisers with the party, of those who vote for it but do not belong to it? One might at first think that these people, being less prejudiced in the party's favour by habit and training, would be even more speedily disillusioned by the undignified spectacles of the last few years. And in some countries that has apparently happened; but not in all. For as the idea of polycentrism has developed, so have certain local communist parties benefited by what, to use a French expression, we could call *enracinement*—a process of 'taking root' in the native soil, or at least of appearing in the public eye to be doing so. This process may or may not go far enough to change the character and strategy of the local party itself; but at least it may go far enough to make the party choose tactics appropriate to its own electoral and other needs, instead of tactics dictated by the Soviet Foreign Ministry. And this may enable the party to do better when elections come. It may, paradoxically, find its own internal organization split and weakened, but its public political leverage strengthened.

But let us get down to some case-by-case analysis. How do you think the dispute would affect parties where this double movement exists and can be observed—in countries, that is, where genuine elections take place and membership figures are published?

SCHAPIRO: France and Italy—these are the clearest cases. But first I should like to make another couple of points about the contrast between élite and mass. One difference between the impact of the dispute on these two is, of course, that the élite hear about it and understand it first; indeed, it may be a long time before the mass is aware of a quarrel at all, and a longer time still before it appreciates the meaning of it.

Secondly, even within the élite of the party we have to distinguish between two types of man—the intellectual and the *apparatchik* pure and simple. For the intellectual, who is in the party because he believes in it, the effect of the Sino-Soviet dispute can be catastrophic; it has taken away the keystone of unity and presented him with a fragile structure. There are two lines being laid down from two centres, there are two popes, two authorities speaking apparently with equal weight yet interpreting the holy scriptures of Marx in diametrically opposed manners.

On the other hand, we find the *apparatchik* who, in his pure culture form at any rate, will accept the most fantastic changes of ideological direction without turning a hair. Now this kind of man is less likely to be daunted even by a split of unprecedented range like the Sino-Soviet one. And thus even where there has been a decline in total party membership, as there has been in Italy and to a slighter extent in France, there is still an effective hard core of apparatus-men who have conducted party activities on behalf of Moscow for years past and look likely, despite all, to do so for years to come if they are given a chance.

Turning then to the mass, there is, as you hinted, a mixed effect. Unity was the great trump card of the communists—the fact that they always spoke with one voice. Now that card has gone, and the effect is certainly divisive and weakening as it must be with any party. Yet, on the other hand, the very existence of the dispute, the very embarrassment of the fact and the very uncertainty as to what new polemic or what new compromise the morrow may bring, forces party spokesmen to talk a little less about Moscow and in terms of Moscow, a little more about and in terms of Italy, or France, or Britain. The mere fact that these spokesmen have to use a language somewhat closer to reality and somewhat further from dogmatism improves the public image of their party and many voters may quickly forget, as voters will, the party's record as agent of a foreign power and begin to be attracted

144

by the sheer vigour of its appeal. That, I should think, is why in Italy, though the membership of the party has somewhat declined, its electoral strength has quite substantially risen.

BURKS: I should like to suggest a slightly different use of the words 'élite' and 'mass'. I quite agree with what has been said on the different impact of the Sino-Soviet dispute on the élite, on the cadres—who will know about its existence much earlier—and on the masses. This difference, implicit anyway in the very nature of an élite contrasted with a mass, is further accentuated by the totalitarian nature of the party.

But in the case of the Italian Party I cannot agree that the decline in its membership has anything to do with the changing morale of its hard core—the intellectuals and the *apparatchiki* that you mentioned. After all, the communist parties have this unique feature of determining, or trying to determine, their own social composition. In their own language, there are two basic types of party, the cadre party which is all élite and no mass, and the mass party with its élite *and* its mass. And the Italian Party is distinctly one of the second, mass type. Of its total membership of something like 1,600,000 at present, the true cadres could hardly exceed—as one Italian party member told me—about 200,000. One eighth of the party, then.

LABEDZ: Yes, we have to be clear whether we are speaking of the mass membership within a party, or of the masses of potential supporters, voters, outside the party.

BURKS: We tend to use the phrase 'communist party' ambiguously. Sometimes we imply the apparatus that runs it, sometimes the rank-and-file as well. This rank-and-file membership I would call an expression of mass support.

SCHAPIRO: Not quite. With a party the size of the Soviet Union's, perhaps, you begin to get something like a mass within the party; but not in Italian conditions. There the pattern is surely the old Leninist one: the cadres at the top control the whole ideological, political and tactical movement; then comes the wider membership who, though not privy to all the inner thoughts and policies of the cadres, are still under discipline and have the job of mobilizing what I would call the mass, the voters. These intermediate ones, the rank-and-file of the party, as in Italy or even France, being under discipline and having jobs to do, are themselves a kind of élite rather than a mass.

BURKS: I would take issue with you on this. I do not think the average member of the Italian Party has a job to do. He goes to cell meetings and the like but, after all, he is not paid.

SCHAPIRO: No, but he *is* under discipline.

BURKS: I agree that there are different degrees of commitment; the mere voter has less commitment than a member of a front organization, a front organization member less than an actual party member, and so on. But after all the communists themselves refer to the Italian Party as a mass party. So, as long as we are clear that we are using words in *their* senses, I think we can usefully distinguish the élite cadres within the party, the mass within the party—when it is the kind of party that has one—and the masses outside the party.

LABEDZ: Well, if we are agreed on this tripartite division, can we now consider the possible effects of the rift upon each section?

SCHAPIRO: Assuming that the aim of a given party remains what it was before—to acquire not merely a share of power but total power—then I should have thought the rift must have a weakening effect both on its élite section and its mass section. Not merely through the direct impact of ideological argument, which can only disturb, I think, a very small number, but chiefly because it opens up to discussion questions of leadership—both present and past—which were never discussed before. And that immediately opens the way for personal feelings about leaders, feelings between leaders and so on, which must act upon the party like the most undesirable sort of yeast, forming a very unpalatable brew. Under the old monolithic system this was not so catastrophic; you could throw away the bad beer, expel the deviationists—and the hard core of reliable loyalists remained. But where there are no certainties the hard core is harder to maintain. So, as I say, if a communist party is geared for the seizure of total power, then the Sino-Soviet dispute reduces its fitness.

BURKS: Precisely—and your point is borne out by a recent (March 1964) meeting at Naples, where the decline in Italian communist membership from 2·1 to 1·6 million was discussed. The party roll has declined in every single year since 1954 except one, 1960. And the cure for this recommended at Naples was—more democracy within the party! More open discussion, less discipline so that new members could be attracted.

LABEDZ: Democracy, in fact, as remedy for the hard core's weakening morale.

SCHAPIRO: And this despite the fact that the effectiveness of the Russian or Chinese Parties, say, in winning revolutions obviously had everything to do with efficient organization but nothing at all to do with internal party democracy. And if this lesson of history is being ignored, is it not because eyes are less firmly fixed upon the Russian and Chinese targets—upon victory in revolution?

And now may I come to the other point, the effect of the rift, and the effect of the new tactics which a given party adopts in response to the rift, upon the masses which it seeks to win over or keep loyal. If you take the Italian and French, and to a certain extent the British Parties' tactics they could be described broadly as what used, in the 'thirties, to be called the 'united front from below'.

These tactics imply that your given communist party concentrates less upon official links with socialists at the top—most socialists being by now rather mistrustful in view of past experience—as upon joint action 'below', like the joint strike action at the Fiat Works in Milan a year or two ago. It can be quite effective for a new-style Italian party official to be able to stand up and say: 'Well, of course, we are the true workers' party. We take no orders from foreigners, but as a matter of fact we stand for the Soviet line which, as you know, is peace, whereas the Chinese stand for war. And incidentally we are a democratic party now'. I do not say that this kind of demagogy will necessarily lead to successful joint action every time, but it certainly seems that that is what the Italian communists are now after—joint action leading to a mass popular front which they would eventually dominate. Joint action, moreover, which would meanwhile undermine the possibility of stable governments of right, left and centre alike, leading to general instability, strikes, street action, and finally the sort of situation in which the Communist Party might hope to come to power. The danger of a chain reaction of this kind occurring in a country with social problems like Italy's is, I should have thought, quite a real one.

BURKS: Perhaps—but we must be clear that the kind of development you are painting is an attempt by a western European communist party to gain mass adherence by legal means as a path to power, not an attempt to seize power by conspiracy from within; this is what your 'united front from below' policy would envisage, if the tactics are now to be democratic—however tongue-in-cheek the feelings they mask.

Secondly, I should like to point out that by-and-large the communist parties of Europe have been losing in electoral strength since

1945, some of them very sharply. The communist share of the poll in Norway, for example, has dropped from 11·9 per cent to 1·8 per cent.

SCHAPIRO: But the French and Italian Parties, since adopting the new tactics, have both gained in electoral support.

BURKS: True, and these are admittedly the biggest ones in western Europe. But there are many more which have lost votes—the Scandinavians, the Swiss, the Greeks, the British. And as for the Italian party, it has gained influence, I consider, by abandoning some of what we would all regard as traditional communist policy, and moving to the right. Even its programme is revisionist: its actual policy, I should say, is more revisionist still. You were saying a minute ago that total power must still be assumed to be the final aim of the communist parties. But in Italian communist literature today you can find references to an opposition that will exist—and be tolerated, apparently—even after communism comes to power.

SCHAPIRO: Is that genuine talk or eye-wash? After all, not only Togliatti but even Thorez used to talk about future 'opposition' under communism.

LABEDZ: The new French party statutes allow for an even more perfect form of internal party democracy, and l'Humanité repeatedly declared that the French communists are against the one-party system. In France, of course.

SCHAPIRO: I am not sure that this is meant sincerely.

BURKS: I am sure it is meant *insincerely*. They hope to get away with it. What *I* am not sure of is whether the conditions of practical politics will allow them to get away with it. At present the Italian Party seems to have only two features that entitle it to be called a 'Marxist-Leninist party of the new type'. One is its apparatus and its system of 'democratic centralism', which is weakening. The other is its foreign policy, inasmuch as it still follows the Soviet lead. But under conditions of polycentrism even that is becoming hesitant. And now we have something unheard of in Stalin's day—the Italian Party trying to form a regional group in western Europe.

SCHAPIRO: Nevertheless there is danger in the present Italian tactics of the 'united front from below'. A brake on dogmatism will improve the party's appeal, and hence the prospect of joint action promoting a

148

broad type of left-wing platform to gather up the protest vote based on various kinds of dissatisfactions in the country. My point was that the communists would hope ultimately to gain control of such a popular front, so that, if they did manage to scale the heights of power, they could use it for purposes quite different from those quoted in their present programme, or from those they would quote when making their popular front alliances.

BURKS: I think this danger exists and I would not want to minimize it. But we must bear in mind that there is also a danger for *them*—the danger that in pursuing such a policy the communists will in fact cease to be a 'party of the new type' and become just another left-wing party: extreme in its doctrinal stand, but more or less democratic in practice.

LABEDZ: As we see, there is a danger *from* the communists in the new situation, and a danger *for* the communists. The danger from the communists is that their popular front tactics may have a measure of success, aided by the fact that the Italian Party, for example, may no longer be so easy to brand as a foreign nationalist party and could, therefore, break out of the political ostracism that has so far been its greatest single obstacle to effective action. On the other hand, the danger *for* them is that under the pressure of events the party—despite all resistance from old cadres—may, by imperceptible degrees, itself succumb to a democratic revolution in its own veins. We should be guilty of dogmatism ourselves if we ruled out that possibility.

So far we have been talking mostly about the big, mass parties in western Europe—the French and Italian. Now if the Sino-Soviet dispute has a weakening effect on the cadres of these mass parties, it must presumably have an even more weakening effect on those parties which are, so to speak, all cadre; parties like the British or the Scandinavian ones which scarcely attract voters at large, but depend on the zealots who remain party members for the same reasons that originally attracted them into it.

BURKS: This is very true. Take the Norwegian party, for example, which is split into three sections. There is the Larsen section . . .

LABEDZ: Larsen?

BURKS: Yes—not the Danish revisionist Larsen—

LABEDZ: I'm sorry, yes—'every Scandinavian is called Larsen except those named Jensen'—a Norwegian was telling me that last week.

BURKS: What was *his* name?

LABEDZ: Christiansen!

BURKS: Ah!—a deviationist. Well, I suppose we can afford to be frivolous about the Norwegian communists, they are rather a pathetic group now.

LABEDZ: Yes, and a convenient illustration of the general rule that the smaller the party, the greater the ideological tension brought about in it by the Sino-Soviet affair; these isolated, last-ditch believers take the ideological argument more seriously than anyone. But won't you complete your enumeration of the Norwegian factions?

BURKS: Larsen's group is cautiously pro-Soviet. Then there is the Loevlien faction, which is anti-revisionist and pro-Chinese. And finally there is Moebekk, leader of what you might call the national communist wing. So the party is well-nigh split into three strips and its paper, *Friheten*, has been carrying pathetic appeals to the Russians not to make life any harder for them by carrying the dispute into the open.

SCHAPIRO: Another feature of the small parties in the developed countries seems to be the growth of disproportionately large Chinese wings, presumably because in such places a revolution seems to be the only thing that could jerk society out of its set ways. There is the Swiss Party....

BURKS: But what are the numbers involved here? Two hundred people at Vevey and fifty at Bienne and there's your Chinese faction. If it weren't for the subsidies they get from the Chinese embassy at Berne they wouldn't exist.

SCHAPIRO: All the same, if the Chinese go on subsidizing them, they may grow.

LABEDZ: Yes, but within very small limits only, determined by the available supply of alienated bohemians and ultra-radical intellectuals of the kind who are everywhere drawn into this sort of marginal political activity.

But perhaps we should now turn to another area, the under-developed countries. There are several ways in which we would expect the impact of the Sino-Soviet dispute to be different there. First of all, the kind of political tactics which influence the masses is different.

The electorate is of another nature entirely. The parties do not have the tradition and organizational coherence of the French or Italian counterparts. In Latin America, of course, there have been communist parties for many years, but in Africa and to some degree in Asia they are mostly post-war phenomena. How do you see the repercussions of the Sino-Soviet split there?

BURKS: Well, I should say that the effect on the mass strength of the parties in under-developed areas seems to have been favourable. Schapiro's warnings about the possibility of the Italian Party turning the dispute to good account would apply even more cogently to these countries. You spoke of the danger of the Italian Party winning an election some day; but look at Indonesia! The government there is scared to hold an election at all for fear that Aidit's Communist Party might win it—as most observers believe it would. There have been no elections since the provincial ones in 1957, when the Communist Party came second in Jakarta and first in two districts of Java. Now one prime reason for the strength of the communists in Indonesia is their position in the Sino-Soviet dispute. For them, it is the Chinese position that best accords with the Indonesian nationalist ambitions to which they must appeal in order to attract votes. The Chinese show sympathy with the Indonesian national goal—necessarily espoused by Aidit too—of opposing Malaysia; and the Indonesian Party in turn joins the Chinese in denouncing 'American imperialism' as the great enemy of mankind.

LABEDZ: At the same time Aidit's position is not simple, because the large Chinese minority in Indonesia is highly unpopular. There is a balance of considerations here.

BURKS: There seem to be three types of situation among the parties of the under-developed world.
One is the situation where the party is distinctly pro-Chinese, with perhaps a small pro-Soviet faction that may indeed have been expelled and is unimportant anyway. This is what you have in Indonesia, Peru and a number of other places.
Then you have the reverse position, with a basically pro-Soviet leadership and membership, though there may be a Chinese faction inside or outside: the Chilean Party comes under this heading.
Thirdly, there is the genuine split into two comparably-sized parts, as in Ceylon.

SCHAPIRO: Since you have mentioned Chile and Peru, I should like your opinion as to why the Peruvian pattern—with the strong pro-

Chinese wing—is not more common in Latin America. I should have expected the Chinese arguments to be more popular in that continent for several reasons—their greater revolutionary appeal, their greater stress on anti-Americanism, and their portrayal of China's economic state as nearer to the Latins' own than the relative advancement the Russians boast of in propagating *their* image.

What the effect of a swing towards China in the Latin American parties would be is a different matter—I should expect it to lead to considerable disorganization and reduced effectiveness.

BURKS: This has already happened to some extent. You have the Cuban prototype and the Chilean, pro-Soviet prototype.

SCHAPIRO: I suppose that the Chilean communists, with their hope of doing well at the next elections, think it would be a foolish time to swap horses.

BURKS: True—but in any case their relations with the Chinese Party are not so bad that they have been broken off completely.

LABEDZ: Meanwhile, they hope to win the elections with their popular front alliance, and the Chinese and their Chilean supporters point out that the last time the Chilean communists did this—back in the 'forties—their partners threw them over as soon as the elections were won.

But to return to the appeal of the Chinese line to Latin Americans: this, I think, has been exaggerated. True, Chinese and Castro-ist lines coincide in favouring the more revolutionary tactics. But I do not believe that Latin Americans enjoy being bracketed together with Africans and Asians as 'under-developed'. Economically their continent obviously is under-developed, but culturally Latin Americans are very conscious of inheriting a European tradition through Spain and Portugal, and of their democratic political institutions, in their case, however prolonged the intervals of dictatorship in so many of the Republics. In face of this sense of sophistication I do not think the Chinese Communist Party can hope to have any great influence in Latin America in the long run.

Of course, there may be certain quick successes where there is a ripe revolutionary situation—but one cannot generalize.

SCHAPIRO: Obviously one would not expect the Chinese to cut any ice in Mexico.

LABEDZ: Nor in Chile, nor in the Argentine.

Now what are the electoral chances of the parties in the various under-developed countries?

BURKS: Chile affords an example of a country which held free elections before and after the Sino-Soviet fracas, in 1961 and in 1963—though the latter ones were only municipal. The communist share of the vote went up from 11·8 to 12·4 per cent. Japan . . .

LABEDZ: Not an under-developed country—

BURKS: No, but a non-European one that affords an interesting comparison with Chile since its party is, by contrast, pro-Chinese—Japan held elections in 1960 and 1963, and the communist percentage of the total vote rose from 3·1 to 4 over the period of the split. Japanese party membership over the same period—to use the more conservative of two independent estimates in the absence of any data from the party itself—increased from 78,000 to 105,000. That of the Minsei front organization, again, was practically quadrupled, and the circulation of the Sunday edition of the communist paper *Akahata* rose three-and-a-half times over those three years.

LABEDZ: I wonder if it is not too early to judge yet. In the past the Japanese Party had been trying to sell itself as 'the lovable party'; but now that it has committed itself to the Peking line, I wonder how it will succeed in combining the soft sell with the hard look! Especially as the Japanese public is so sensitive on the test-ban issue.

BURKS: You are right, it may be too early. But I must point out that in another part of Asia, Aidit is very effectively combining, as you put it, the soft sell and the hard look—a revisionist domestic line and an aggressive pro-Peking foreign policy. And though you may think the 1963 elections in Japan came too early to register the full impact of the rift, yet the public was after all faced at these same elections with a breakaway group of pro-Soviet communists—former members of the leadership who had left in July 1961 and founded a separate, short-lived party.

SCHAPIRO: Of course, the French and Italian Parties, over the same period again, showed much bigger electoral increases than your Chileans and Japanese. In fact the French almost doubled their cantonal representation, from 50 to 99.

153

BURKS: Well, I would be cautious about interpreting cantonal elections. The Italian Party, it is true, has improved its voting share of the total electorate from 22·6 per cent to 25·3 per cent over the ten years up to 1963; but that is not nearly as big an increase as the Japanese communists' advance from 3·1 per cent to 4 per cent in only three years. In other words, I don't think we have the figures to prove that western parties in general have benefited more, in votes, from the rift than the eastern ones.

LABEDZ: To recapitulate, then, we all agree that the electoral chances of the well-established communist parties cannot be expected to wither away, as some optimists imagined, purely because polycentrism has entered the stage. On the contrary, they may improve because many a former tactical shackle which made a party slave to the vagaries of Soviet policy has now disappeared.

BURKS: I think we should be happy to accept the risk that some parties may have better electoral chances, if we gain the dissolution of the world communist movement as an organization operating from a single centre.

SCHAPIRO: I will make that bargain too. For the danger from international communism has always lain in its discipline and organization; those gone, its main menace has disappeared in the long run. Even in countries like Italy, where the party may now strike a more genuinely popular root than before, it will take a long time to live down its old-style record.

LABEDZ: And beyond that, the party—in Italy and elsewhere—may itself be affected by the polycentric process, and nobody can tell precisely how.

SCHAPIRO: Which is exactly the Chinese grudge against the Russians. I think the Chinese are right!

10
Prospects

SPEAKERS

Robert Conquest

Richard Lowenthal

Leopold Labedz

10. Prospects

LABEDZ: In most of the discussions that have made up this series we have been chiefly concerned with the short-term effects of the Sino-Soviet split upon the various communist countries and communist parties. But I should like today's session to be devoted to long-range effects; to the bearing of the dispute upon such perennial party concerns as ideology and policy...

CONQUEST: ...whether ideology determines policy, or vice versa, to put it cynically...

LABEDZ: That's the sort of thing, yes....And then the long-range effects of the dispute, if any, in changing the nature of the parties themselves—the roles they aim to play in their various societies, the doctrines they invoke to justify those aims and to prove their special fitness to accomplish them...

CONQUEST: The question of party legitimation, in fact.

LABEDZ: And that is of course a question of redoubled import in this 'post-split era'; for each party has to justify itself not only *vis-à-vis* the domestic public, but also *vis-à-vis* other communist parties. And then, finally, the effect of the dispute on the kind of personalities who will step on to the stage of communist history.

To start off with Conquest's cynical point about ideology and policy, my own view is likewise that the *direct* effects of ideology upon the political decisions of the parties are all but nil. Ideology is nevertheless very important because it has indirect effects: communist leaders who have been nurtured on a diet of ideological clichés obviously show the results of that nutriment when they later come to make political choices. And their parties have always regurgitated those clichés—a process known as quoting from the classics of Marxism-Leninism—as the most thought-saving and irrefutable way of proving that they are on the right lines. The fact that we now increasingly find communist parties in different countries quoting from the same classics to prove opposite points...

CONQUEST: ...or even two communist parties in the same country doing so....

LABEDZ: Yes—this fact adds to the fun for us unsympathetic outsiders, but it has not so far led to the practice being dropped. Of course, we must not think of 'national communism' as being a development of the last few years. From the start, wherever Marxism took root, it has been affected by the native milieu, the historical context of a given country; and so we get a German Marxism, a Russian Marxism, an Austro-Marxism, an Italian Marxism, not to mention that strange blend of Marxism with Confucianism and Taoism which is known as Maoism. The process of polycentrism in the communist movement will presumably accelerate this 'naturalization' of Marxism in different countries.

LOWENTHAL: I'm afraid you have given us a very richly piled platter of subjects to get our teeth into. But let me try and crack this first nut you offered us—the sincerity of communist ideology. Of course I agree with you that communists do not look up the book whenever they are confronted by a new situation. But I do think they are motivated by a fundamental faith which they hold seriously—what may be called 'Leninist faith'. And what we are experiencing during this Sino-Soviet dispute, as far as it affects ideology, is, I suggest, a disintegration of Leninism into its two component parts. Let me explain.

Lenin transformed classical Marxism to suit the conditions of an under-developed country, as Russia then was, and to suit his belief in the immediacy of world revolution. So he laid much *less* stress than Marx on economic maturity as a precondition for socialism, and much *more* stress than Marx on revolutionary determination, on the necessity to act now, to mobilize in fact even colonial peoples in countries where there was hardly any industry and so hardly any proletariat.

Leninism is thus a kind of false synthesis between certain Marxian ideas about the future development of industrial society, and the very Russian urge for immediate revolution. And now, in this Sino-Soviet dispute, we find the Russians increasingly stressing the Marxist requirement of economic maturity and reliance on industrial proletariats —the very arguments the Mensheviks once used against the Bolsheviks!—while the Chinese emphasize the revolutionary determination of the peoples of Asia, Africa and Latin America—the role, to use Toynbee's term, of the external proletariat of the West.

LABEDZ: What Lenin did was to make a synthesis between Marx's economic determinism and the tradition of the Narodniki, the Populists, with their belief in agrarian revolution.

158

CONQUEST: I should be inclined to call the second element in Lenin's synthesis not Populist but Blanquist; after all, the Populists rejected *political* revolution as playing into the hands of the bourgeoisie; I should say the earlier French group under Louis Blanqui with its call for a professional revolutionary élite—these were surely Lenin's other precursors.

LABEDZ: Well, you may argue for both ancestors in respect of Lenin.

CONQUEST: And in respect of the Chinese too, who have achieved in their own fashion the Populist aim of a peasant-based revolution, but who, like Louis Blanqui, see the revolution as the product of the party's will-power above all.

LABEDZ: Agreed. But the point I wished to make was this: that whereas in Lenin's day the embarrassing cleavage between Marx's proletarian formula and the Populist, or Blanquist, enthusiasm for immediate action could be veiled over by Russia's intermediate status. . . .

CONQUEST: You mean her status as a country backward, yet still possessed of a flourishing nucleus of industrialization. . . .

LABEDZ: Precisely—and now, in Khrushchev's day, that veiling over is not possible: there is a stark contrast between a highly industrialized Russia and the underdeveloped countries whose revolutionary interests China claims to espouse. There is a corresponding contrast between a Russian ideology stressing the old Menshevik-Marxist elements, and a Chinese one stressing the voluntarist, act-now elements in the Leninist mixture.

But how free, now, are the Russian leaders to act in accordance with the trend of their own ideology? They are not, of course, inhibited by fear of being called to account in parliamentary fashion.

CONQUEST: No, but they may be inhibited by the facts they have to face. Khrushchev has to face the facts of the agricultural situation, say, and, broadly speaking, the ideology of collectivism is incompatible with the practical need for modernization. The *apparatchiki* may be backward but the top-level leaders manage to drag them slowly along with them.

LOWENTHAL: Yes, I agree that the Soviet leaders are trying to yield to the pressure of circumstances and to modernize the country—

within certain limits. And the limits are set by the need to preserve a coherent ideology, since this must be maintained in order to legitimize the very system of one-party rule. The real question, then, is how the cadres' faith in the party's ideology is weakened by the Sino-Soviet split; and if anything it has shown that loyalty to international communism is not strong enough to outweigh a conflict of nationalities.

Moreover, this has not even been the first major blow, but the third, following de-Stalinization and then the Hungarian revolution. All these major blows to the faith, to the ideology of communism, are likely to make it more and more difficult to reassert the primacy of the party over the various Soviet élites—administrative, economic, technical, military—when these get a chance to contest that primacy, as they did in the crisis after Stalin's death and may well do again in the next succession crisis. It seems to me that the top party leaders are well aware of that problem: since the central committee plenum of November 1962, Khrushchev has been trying to shift the emphasis from the party's ideological-political role to its alleged economic calling, has quoted Lenin as witness that after the conquest of power the chief tasks are economic, and has sought to reorganize the party so as to make each party secretary directly responsible for a sector of production. It is as if the Soviet communists were wondering whether they could not replace the justification of their rule by faith—a faith that is so visibly waning—by a justification by works, by economic achievement. Even such an arch-ideologist as Suslov has gone so far —in his report on the Chinese schism to the central committee meeting of February 1964—as to say that the principal *international* duty of the Soviet communists is to build communism at home so as to encourage communists everywhere by its example; after 'socialism in one country', this is 'communism in one empire'! But there is a weakness in this type of justification for party rule: it makes sense that you need a party dictatorship to sustain a permanent ideological conflict with the outside world, but it is not very convincing that you must have a party dictatorship in order to produce more food, more shoes or more houses. Moreover, while the hope of goulash may be more attractive to the modern Soviet citizen than the hope of world revolution, the promise of 'goulash tomorrow', if not fulfilled, loses its credibility very much quicker than that of 'world revolution tomorrow'.

LABEDZ: But even without that problem the Soviet leadership is already in a chronic dilemma over its commitment to an outdated ideology. Internally, it is simply a choice between adherence to ideology and modernization, or so it may seem to the more intelligent and impatient leaders. But with every step they make toward modernization they make themselves vulnerable to external attacks by the Chinese and others who can rightly object that such moves are 'not in the book', that they do not conform with the Marxist classics, that they are revisionist. The real reasons for modernization—the desire of the Russian leaders, urged on by the technocrats' advice, to make Russia efficient and strong—are a matter of relative indifference to the critics.

Now a similar situation of conflict between ancient commitment to a doctrine and the exigencies of contemporary life, between power and ideology, can arise for any communist party which is strong enough to be concerned with power at all, and not simply with doctrinal quibbling. So let us consider some of these cases where the power-versus-ideology dilemma really affects a party in regard to its domestic legitimation and, externally, to its position in the international movement.

CONQUEST: The party that comes first to my mind is the Polish, simply because it has gone so far in discarding collectivization in practice—and done so little to discard it in theory.

LOWENTHAL: Yes, but the Polish reforms contradicting or ignoring doctrine go back, do they not, to 1956 and reflect, not a general crisis of ideology such as we are discussing, but the reality of Polish needs plus a crisis in Soviet authority brought about by an earlier shock than the Sino-Soviet dispute—by de-Stalinization. If we are speaking of the Soviet bloc countries, then their main reaction to the *present* dispute is surely this: they are trying to exploit it in order particularly to increase their freedom of movement further still, and to escape subjection to the planned division of labour directed from Moscow. What I find exceedingly difficult to forecast is whether they will succeed in these tactics once the dispute goes a stage further and there is an open excommunication of the Chinese. I suspect that when this open breach has taken place the Russians will try to tighten up discipline a little more again, and that this is why many of the east European revisionists —or semi-demi-revisionists—are afraid of a complete rupture. They like the present situation because it affords them a little more scope for manoeuvre.

However, it is quite possible that in the long run discipline will *not* be tightened up. Nationalism has on the whole become stronger throughout the communist world, even in countries which were communized on Soviet bayonets. Year by year the satellites have become a little less satellite, a little stronger in relation to the USSR, irrespective of the dispute with China.

But let us look beyond the Soviet bloc at the major communist parties outside, at a pro-Soviet one like the Italian or a pro-Chinese one like Indonesia's, to take the two strongest. What we find there is not just an erosion of ideology and increased pressure for modernization, but a general reappraisal of each party's relation to the international movement. For if the old centre of the movement, Moscow, is no longer unique—and however pro-Soviet you are you cannot claim that—then you cannot with a clear conscience justify, as communists used to, the attitude 'My Soviet Union, right or wrong'. And the Italian communists, in fact, have stopped trying to justify it. Indeed, they occasionally try to show that they too can be critical; and even the French Party sometimes makes little flapping gestures as if it, too, would like to show some independence. If such things are possible, then something has happened to the substance of the communist faith in these countries, which has for some decades past been anchored to the Soviet Union.

CONQUEST: It's old experience that Marxism is susceptible of endless interpretations, like any other doctrine claiming to be a repository of truth. No amount of definition, as such, does any good. The narrowest of Marxists, as of Christian sects, remains equally subject to internal heresy and schism. Only the existence of a final authority, whose decisions are binding, can prevent a certain disintegration. The present position is that for the communists of a given country the decisions of its own central committee are still binding, but that the hierarchical links between the parties have broken down. It is difficult to see how they could be renewed. It would require the revival of a clear-cut dogmatism, involving almost certainly one-man-rule in the Soviet Union. Such a development is by no means impossible. But even that would not be enough. It would next be necessary, in the case of the other parties, to 'compel them to come in'. But—except for a few cases, like perhaps the French—it is difficult to see even the most dogmatic and Stalinist of the non-Soviet parties sacrificing their autonomy, that is giving up any part of the power now held by the leaderships.

The basic problem of neo-Stalinism in Russia would be that of reducing eastern Europe to order, and China to the more or less amicable pretence at obedience—'say one, do other'—of Stalin's time; (in that case, no doubt, the 'outside' parties could come to heel or be replaced by similar but more loyal groups). Now, some sort of arrangement with the Chinese might, in the circumstances, not be too difficult. But for eastern Europe it would be a question of coups organized by the Russians in favour of ambitious groups opposed to the leaderships and willing to trade independence for power—the sort of thing the Russians attempted in Albania a couple of years ago. On the face of it, this would be an extraordinarily difficult task. Yet if pursued flexibly enough, it might not be quite impossible. After Gomulka's death, even Poland could conceivably be reduced, if the appearances were preserved rather better than in Stalin's time. In Bulgaria, the current leadership—opposed by all the real forces of the party, left and right— could probably be forced to come to heel. Even so, it is difficult to envisage complete success. Just the same, it is fairly clear that even the present Russian régime only tolerates diversity on the calculation as a lesser evil. If it led to total disintegration, they might think again.

LABEDZ: The crisis of ideology and the crisis of authority are in fact inseparable. The erosion of ideology is undermining authority—the authority of the old centre *vis-à-vis* the satellites within the world movement, or the authority of local party leaders *vis-à-vis* their members and *vis-à-vis* outsiders.

To take the first element: the Soviet leadership is no longer a centre of authority; it has to fight to justify its position. Whatever it does is subject to the scrutiny—still very tentative and modest—of other communist parties; but we can expect that these parties will become bolder in future and not limit themselves to such marginal targets of comment as Khrushchev's views on abstract art, criticized by the Italians; or his attitude to the Jews, criticized by the French communists. Conceivably, these parties may take up critical positions on politically more substantive issues and decisions, and this could create, instead of one single Sino-Soviet dispute, a whole host of disputes running through the international movement. This in turn would mean that no single party could hope to prevail in all cases on its own; and that in turn would create a habit of seeking coalitions, making regional agreements and so on. Each party that set out on this course would find itself having to manœuvre hard within the movement, and not merely to steer left or right of the Sino-Soviet reef.

The second kind of authority that is being undermined, as I said, is the authority of the local party in its own country....

LOWENTHAL: You are referring to parties in power?

LABEDZ: For the moment, yes. The weakening of the ideological basis of their authority, as a result of the various blows you mentioned and now as a result of the Sino-Soviet dispute, means that the parties in power must search for some new, post-Stalin legitimation for one-party rule. What new basis of support can they find?

LOWENTHAL: Yes, this problem is—or will be—very real in Russia herself. If, during another succession crisis, leaders arise who want to push the party somewhat into the background, they will, I think, have a stronger position than Malenkov did when he tried to do something of the sort after Stalin's death.

But the problem is most immediate for some of the great communist parties outside the bloc which want to get back into the swim of the actual development of society, as against the copybook analyses of what Marx or Lenin said *ought* to happen. Think of the Italians, who do not want to be isolated any more, and who in order to get back into the swim must erase the impression that they are a mere tool of Russia —must indeed erase all traces of the fact itself, for they most sincerely do not want to be such a tool.

CONQUEST: The effort is complicated for them by the fact that on such issues as the inevitability of war they must—to 'be in the swim', as you say, of public esteem—be definitely on the Russian side of the argument with China. . . .

LOWENTHAL: Oh yes; they still regard Russia as a great friend, as a model in some ways, and in general they support her on foreign policy issues. But they must be rid of the necessity of supporting Russia in everything, unconditionally; and they must be seen to be rid of it.

As for their internal organization, the character of their party machine and so on, they are becoming a little doubtful as to whether, even for them, the right road to power is the Leninist road. They are very friendly with the Yugoslavs, who have been saying ever since 1954 that communist party rule is, perhaps, the right thing for some countries but not for all. And now the Italians are beginning to say that if their party won, it would allow other parties to exist; it would form a coalition; and it would even allow an opposition to exist.

You may say these are all tactical promises and would not be kept in the event. But how long will they remain merely tactical? They are being made, remember, in an atmosphere of internal party discussion more free-ranging than anything that any communist party has experienced for years past! Debate is allowed which implies revision of the whole communist picture of the development of modern industrial capitalism. The idea that non-communist industrial societies are at their last gasp, as Stalin usually assumed, is now being rejected as utterly unrealistic. Well, what the Italians started as an exercise in tactical adaptation to a new situation may go well beyond the tactical intentions of its initiators.

CONQUEST: What is more, the Italians have actually allowed public debate of a heretical—or at least dubious—nature as between members of their own hierarchy, and not merely their intellectual hangers-on. Tactically speaking, Western parties might find themselves no longer acting as communist parties are supposed to do at all, but becoming little more than left-wing socialist parties. This is the impression that Togliatti and others are trying to give. But it will only be an appearance so long as 'democratic centralism' prevails. So long as the party retains this communist version of the *Führerprinzip*, then its aim of sole, and hence terrorist, one-party rule remains decisive. But if these first stirrings of genuine inner-party democracy led to the position achieved only once by a communist party—the Hungarian under Nagy—then the communists would have begun to re-enter civilised political life, and the long epoch of totalitarian sectarianism (for which Lenin is to blame) would have broken down, at least locally. But this seems rather a long-term hope.

LABEDZ: Yes, this is one prospect for a strong, but not ruling, party in an industrial country; it has to modernize its theories and aspirations to keep pace with changing facts and changing convictions and preferences among its potential supporters, just as the ruling parties have to modernize their actual practices to keep pace with changing needs. Now what of the non-ruling parties in non-industrial, under-developed countries?

LOWENTHAL: The most important of these is, of course, the Indonesian—at least it is the largest. The ironical thing about these is that polycentrism and fragmentation may not be harming their chances of victory, but helping them. For the Indonesian communist it is not, I think, terribly important whether he should look to Moscow or Peking for doctrinal guidance. What is important to him is that his country is in a great muddle and that he believes, and can persuade others, that the Communist Party is the only one with a clear plan for straightening out the muddle.

CONQUEST: Yes, we have a kind of prototype for such countries in Cuba. If Castro had been fully and obviously under Russian control he would never have attained power.

LABEDZ: Quite—and one result of the polycentric trend is that Castro is now unlikely ever to come under exclusive Russian control, just as in what used to be called satellite countries communist leaders formerly under Russian control are now escaping from it. Ex-Stalinists and anti-Stalinists and Castrists alike—they are all enjoying a greater margin for the expression of their own, authoritarian, nationalist leanings.

LOWENTHAL: Nationalist—and personal authoritarian leanings.

LABEDZ: Quite—and this question of the role of personalities in determining history, though a rather hackneyed one in the tradition of Marxist polemics, is one that has to be asked again whenever a fresh context arises that makes single, individual decisions fateful.

LOWENTHAL: And the present-day growth of autonomous totalitarian parties is just such a fresh context. I quite agree with you that the process of polycentric decay may unloose the forces of local, national totalitarianism in some countries. In fact I would say this is likely whenever two conditions are fulfilled: first, that there is a domestic situation objectively favourable to revolution—a situation we scarcely find in western Europe today, but certainly do find for example in Indonesia; and secondly, that there should be able totalitarian leaders available. The factor of personality is extremely obvious here but none the less crucial. No revolutionary crisis *necessarily* leads to a totalitarian solution. It leads to it when the anti-totalitarian forces are not able to produce an alternative solution, and when there is a totalitarian party on the spot, well enough led to make full use of its opportunities.

LABEDZ: Or—perhaps we should add, in order to cover the Cuban case—when there is a potentially totalitarian party plus a forceful leader. . . .

LOWENTHAL: But I think Castro is too exceptional a case to provide a typical pattern.

CONQUEST: Yes, and Castro's stability—or the stability of a totalitarian régime in Indonesia—seems dubious.

LABEDZ: Well, let us try to delve below the level of mere accident and consider what kinds of society are likely to produce the sort of leader you have described as essential for totalitarian development —the strong personality able to forge power in times of crisis and retain it afterwards. If we compare the social backgrounds of the

Russian revolution and the Chinese revolution with Castro's revolution, I think we can see some common patterns. Very broadly speaking we find at an early stage a pre-revolutionary intelligentsia, tender-hearted, sentimental and visionary; and later the emergence of a more ruthless type of intelligentsia, like the *Raznochintsy* in Russia, who are both ruthless and tough-minded. But this is 1960, not 1860 or 1870, and characteristics have changed considerably; for all that, we still apply the Russian word 'intelligentsia' to this heterogeneous social grouping in the underdeveloped countries which includes students, ex-students, unfinished students, not-quite-begun students—

LOWENTHAL: —young officers—

LABEDZ: ... and these are of course a long way removed from the Chekhov type with pince-nez. Nor are they ex-priests from the seminaries; this is a new, 'third world' intelligentsia. Perhaps they have more in common with nineteenth-century Russians of the Nechaev type, Bakunin's disciple who wrote a *Revolutionary Catechism* for the guidance of conspirators—

LOWENTHAL: I should say they are a cross between some of the Bolshevik types and some of the Nazi types.

LABEDZ: And that is why they shift so easily from one type of movement to the other.

CONQUEST: Yes. And I think there is an interesting parallel in the half-baked 'quasi-intellectual' atmosphere of the two parties. Throughout the history of the Soviet Communist Party one finds crackpot ideas very reminiscent of the sort of stuff talked in the Vienna cafés before the First War among Hitler and his like: Lysenkoism for example. One is reminded of Lenin's remark to Gorky, that he should avoid Bolshevik doctors at all costs and go to a bourgeois one: he knew that the former would be crackpots.

LOWENTHAL: Since we are talking of types, there is an interesting contrast of types now coming to the surface among the communists in Latin America. One such type is the professional party *apparatchik* who has for many years helped to run a party without any hope of seizing power, and without much thought of trying. Another is the type of man like Castro's right hand, Ché Guevara, who has a Marxist ideological background but is primarily a man of instant revolutionary action who comes to the fore in a revolutionary situation.

LABEDZ: So we see that the effect of a particular social background on the character of a communist party and on the character of its leadership is going to be all the more conspicuous during a period of fragmentation and growing autonomy, and this must make the rifts within the movement deeper in their turn. In some countries we shall still be finding the old type of bohemian turned into an armed intellectual; what a contrast with, say, Italy where party cadres may even come to be recruited from the ranks of perfectly respectable citizens. I think we are witnessing the first occasion in the history of the communist movement when differences of social background may have a serious political effect on it.

LOWENTHAL: I think you are right. There is now no international centralism to hold things together. There is no longer a world party; in fact, there is no longer world communism in the classical sense. The prospects for communism are quite different in different parts of the world; they always were, of course, but the contrasts and the reasons are both becoming clearer.

LABEDZ: And what are those prospects in the industrial West?

LOWENTHAL: Of political victory—none, I should say. As the parties in the advanced countries become more loosely organized and less totalitarian, their intellectual contribution may become more interesting —a brand of more independent-minded Marxism could evolve—but their chances of power will become less. Their revisionist, more realistic, Marxism might make once again the kind of genuine contribution to some social science which Marxism stopped doing in Stalin's day; but it will no longer make a decisive contribution to the political life of the Western nations.

In the underdeveloped countries, by contrast, we may get powerful, Leninist parties in which the Marxist and internationalist elements become progressively less important but whose chances of power still remain considerable. I am thinking less of Africa than of Asia and the Middle East, where there are real mass movements—

LABEDZ: —and where the weakness of institutional developments gives any existing organization a better chance to manipulate the relatively undifferentiated, incoherent masses.

CONQUEST: The chances of communism in these countries—or of totalitarian movements in general—are surely enhanced also by the absence of a tradition of public political discourse about real issues.

LOWENTHAL: Yes, but the specific advantage of the West is not the tradition of discussion as such, but the tradition of people organizing for the steady representation of their interests.

LABEDZ: Organizing pluralistically.

CONQUEST: But the tradition of organization leads to the tradition of sophistication, doesn't it? Of sophisticated expectations and sophisticated talk. So that what Russians would call quite a 'backward' worker in Britain or France, say, one who has not the slightest notion of what kind of utopia he would prefer, has a pretty clear notion of what he can reasonably expect now. He will fight like a fiend to get his 4 per cent wage increase, but if you told him 'You need 10 per cent, good man!' he would shrug his shoulders and say 'Nonsense, of course we don't. 10 per cent isn't possible'.

And of course this goes with considerable scepticism about grand long-term promises on the part of political leaders. Millenarian sects appeal only to a tiny minority. Even communist parties, in the western countries, spend most of their time pretending to be interested only in short-term aims. Moreover, where political sophistication and scepticism are prevalent among the population, the intellectuals do not play much of a role. In the East, it is a question of persuading a few thousand students that totalitarianism will industrialize their country quickest. They then feed various simple cover stories to the masses, obtaining control of their rather primitive organizations without enormous difficulty, in the absence of other literate *cadres*. In Russia, in 1917, the masses were on the whole cut off from the body politic and thus manipulable in something of the same way—and it was, in addition, a time of great instability. Russia is now, potentially at least, much more mature: apart from the primitive *apparatchik* mind, there seems to be considerable receptivity to common sense and pragmatic argument, and resistance to pie in the sky.

LABEDZ: And so, in a roundabout way, the Sino-Soviet conflict seems likely amongst many other things to contribute to a widening of the gulf between the developed and the underdeveloped countries, by helping to differentiate the communist parties in these two types of countries, leading them to adopt contrasting attitudes toward a much wider range of subjects than the Sino-Soviet dispute itself, and leading them to acquire diverging characters altogether.

This, of course, is only one element in a much bigger picture, and that picture is the end of an epoch—the end of the age of unity in the international communist movement. For the unity of ideology is at an end; the unity of political action is at an end. Galloping autonomy —polycentrism—will ensure that the various parties are far more influenced than heretofore by their various national environments.

But—one last question. How long will it be before the historic character of these facts, the essential newness of the situation, are grasped by the communists themselves? For how long will they try to conceal the reality from people's eyes, even from their own eyes, by rationalizing it into verbiage, weaving it into a new myth, varnishing it with gobbledygook?

LOWENTHAL: Why, of course, we must not underestimate their gobbledygook. But how long it will take for people to see through the varnish—to realise that what the communists are doing in one part of the world is fundamentally different from what they are doing, what they will be doing, in another—that is a different matter. We started, did we not, with this distinction between the Marxist element in communist doctrine and the later, specifically Leninist element—a distinction that throws grave doubt upon that hyphen in the official term *Marxism-Leninism*. Well—perhaps not so grave after all. The two elements have one important attribute in common—irrelevance.

LABEDZ: Irrelevance? To what?

LOWENTHAL: That is the point of my question. How long, I wonder, will it be before the world at large discovers the basic irrelevance of Marxism to the underdeveloped countries, and the basic irrelevance of Leninism to the advanced ones?

II

After Khrushchev

SPEAKERS

Hugh Seton-Watson

Melvin J. Lasky

Leopold Labedz

11. After Khrushchev

LABEDZ: Since we spoke last, the long-drawn drama of communist history has been interrupted by another curtain-drop: the curtain dropped in front of Khrushchev, and when it rose again he had been whisked away into the wings. So we have to consider how this event has changed, or will change, the Sino-Soviet confrontation—

LASKY:—if at all—

LABEDZ:—if at all, granted; and secondly what the impact of the switch in Soviet leadership will be on an East Europe in which the quarrel with Peking has already started a new ferment. First, then, how the dismissal has affected the rift itself. So far it does not look as if negotiations between Mr. Chou En-lai and Mr. Brezhnev have brought about any real change in Sino-Soviet relations.

LASKY: Was there any serious effort to heal the breach? Was there any, so to speak, communist goodwill on each side? Was there indeed any during previous attempts to patch things up?

SETON-WATSON: I suppose they have tried from time to time. But each time they found it had got harder.

LASKY: And what were these obstacles that have seemed to get larger each time? At one time in the dispute the adversaries did not even mention names, or only secondary names like Albania and Yugoslavia, but not the names of the principals. Later they mentioned the true names, but not the real issues.

LABEDZ: I would rather say that they did mention the real issues, but cast them in such a doctrinal form that only the initiated could see how profound the differences between the parties were. But genuine enough issues *were* mentioned. Foreign policy, for example, in relation to America and in relation to the under-developed countries. In the end, even territorial issues between Russia and China.

SETON-WATSON: Yes, the foreign policy issues I would have thought were the basic ones. The Chinese have got to the point where they insist on supremacy in Asia for themselves. They expect the Soviet Union to give them complete backing to do whatever they want about India, whatever they want about Japan. I am sure the Chinese find one thing in Asia insufferable, and that is the Soviet influence over Indonesia. They have to give some propaganda support, of course, to the confrontation policy against Malaysia; but it is Russia, not China, has been encouraging Soekarno's adventurism. The common idea that the Soviet Union is everywhere moderate and peace-loving, and China aggressive and violent, is far from the truth in Asia. In their own vicinity the Chinese can often be quite moderate, as they have been towards say Cambodia and Burma, and quite slow to incite, as in Indonesia, where the Russians are doing the arming and the egging on. The Soviet presence in Indonesia, or in India, must be almost as unacceptable to Peking as a western imperialist presence. It seems to me that they have got to the point where they will not tolerate Soviet influence in Asia, and this is a point where I cannot see the Soviets giving way. Here, at least, the room for manœuvre is surely nil for both sides.

LASKY: But surely it is Chinese militancy which the Russians have found embarrassing for their foreign policy, especially *vis-à-vis* the United States and in Europe.

SETON-WATSON: I did not mean to suggest that the picture was everywhere the same. In most of Asia the Chinese are moderate because it is they who have to pay the price. The Russians, by contrast, can afford to be extreme in Indonesia because that is a long way from their own frontiers. But nearer the Soviets' home base—in the Middle East or even Africa, and certainly in Europe—it is the Chinese who advocate violence and the Russians who are more careful. In Latin America, a long way from both Peking and Moscow, they can both perhaps afford to be adventurous, as long as the adventure is not too close to the USA: Cuba has taught Moscow a lesson.

LABEDZ: The distance-proportional-to-militancy rule seems to fail over Vietnam. After all it was Peking that castigated Moscow over pussy-footing in Tonkin Bay...

SETON-WATSON: No, I don't think Vietnam disproves my point, because the Chinese have really had no freedom of choice there. They are not supporting the Vietminh because of any regular preference for militant policies. The war was already on in 1949 when the Chinese got to the frontier and they have been involved in it ever since. But the 'adventurism' and risk-taking are the work of the North Vietnam communists.

Chinese denunciation of the Russians for not being tough with the Americans over the Tonkin Bay affair can also be seen, I think, as a twinge from an old wound, one of the sorest spots in Sino-Soviet relations. And that was the Russians' complete abandonment of China over Formosa. Just when the Formosan issue began to get acute, Khrushchev saw fit to go and parley with Eisenhower at Camp David. That I am sure was a traumatic moment for communist China.

LABEDZ: Yes, and Khrushchev was the villain. Perhaps when he was pushed off the stage Peking hoped that the whole play might take a turn for the better——

LASKY: ——or indeed assumed that he had been pushed off the stage for that very reason, *in order* that relations with China should improve——

LABEDZ: ——and yet on both sides things continued to be done that made such a *dénouement* impossible. On the very day Chou En-lai was in Moscow celebrating the anniversary of the Bolshevik Revolution —7 November 1964—the new pro-Chinese communist party in India was set up. Then, after some hesitation, the Russians gave their blessing to the Shiga-Suzuki group to form a pro-Soviet breakaway party in Japan. While this process of schismatic development goes on between the respective Asian supporters of Russian and Chinese policies, how can one expect the Russians and Chinese themselves to shake hands again?

SETON-WATSON: There is an intriguing possibility that arises in this connection. We have often seen in these talks how, in the Soviet bloc proper, the East European communist parties have gained greater freedom of manoeuvre, greater bargaining power, *vis-à-vis* Moscow because of Moscow's own difficulties with Peking. Stalin could simply give orders to the Rumanian or the Czechoslovak Party; Khrushchev has had to purchase their obedience at a certain price. And the European parties outside the bloc, particularly the Italians, have been able to a certain extent to exert the same sort of leverage. Now I wonder whether in Asia today the parties on the Chinese side of the fence are able to obtain concessions in return for the support they give to Peking in the international quarrel? If so, a further question arises. If Moscow and Peking are each being bled by their own leeches, does this simply weaken each of them, or does it on the contrary give them a fellow-feeling and encourage whatever desire they have to come to terms and recover full control over their subordinates?

LABEDZ: Well, how much symmetry is there in this respect between Moscow and Peking? First of all, Peking only has two satellites in the Soviet-bloc sense, namely North Korea and North Vietnam, and

North Vietnam does not really qualify even so. Then you have got the pro-Chinese parties in India, Ceylon and so on, but they can scarcely be said to be 'bleeding' the Chinese Party as the East European parties 'bleed' Moscow ...

LASKY: Because they are not ruling parties.

SETON-WATSON: Well, the Indonesian Party for one seems well within reach of power and is surely in a position to bargain with Peking.

LABEDZ: They could if anybody could, I admit, and all the more effectively because of the vast economic and military aid they have had from Russia. Or rather the aid Soekarno has had from Russia, I should say. And it remains to be seen whether Aidit—if the Indonesian communists come to power—can juggle two balls more successfully than Soekarno in his heyday juggled three.

LASKY: With American aid as the third, you mean?

LABEDZ: Quite. But since Seton-Watson has brought us round to Eastern Europe again, let's for a moment reconsider the situation there since Khrushchev's fall. Before that event, you remember, our general judgment was that it was in the interest of the ruling communist parties there to have the Sino-Soviet conflict continue, but not to see a total break. Reconciliation, on the other hand, would restrict their field of manœuvre. Has this position changed?

LASKY: Isn't that formula of yours an over-statement? Except for the Rumanians, has any Eastern European party really utilized the Sino-Soviet conflict to do any manœuvring? Have the Poles, the Czechs, the East Germans? ...

SETON-WATSON: Oh yes, I think it is clear that the conflict has usually enabled a party to do more what its leaders wanted and less what Moscow wanted, though that did not necessarily mean a move towards liberalism. For the Hungarians, it did bring more domestic freedom. The Bulgarian Party, on the contrary, wanted to be tougher and used their greater freedom of manœuvre to be so. Then, ironically, it was Khrushchev who forced through certain modifications, by backing Zhivkov against Yugov and others. Poland is different again. There I suppose the trend for some years has been towards tougher and more unpleasant policies at home; but this, I should have thought, was Gomulka's wish rather than Moscow's.

However, it is the particular impact of Khrushchev's fall that we are asked to consider now. Well, the struggle for the succession has only just begun and all historical precedent suggests we are in for a lengthy period of weakness in the Soviet leadership. A period of manœuvring and demagogy and internal propaganda, both within the Soviet Party and, probably, within the international movement as a whole. One of the factors in the succession struggle in Moscow may well be the views of outside communist parties, and rival candidates for power will have to take account of them as one pressure group, even if not the most potent pressure group, in the game.

Again, just as the prospective successors to Khrushchev will have an interest in offering competitive concessions to leaders of outside communist parties—the big non-ruling ones like the French and Italian as well as the satellite ones—so these leaders themselves, faced with succession questions or with internal rivalries, will try to make play with their influential connection in Moscow.

LABEDZ: Precisely. The schismatic tendency filters downward and then seeps back again; take the struggle in Czechoslovakia around Novotny, or the struggle between the various Polish party factions, the possible struggles which may continue in Bulgaria even after the defeat of the Stalinist remnant.

SETON-WATSON: Yes, cliques will form inside the 'satellite' parties roughly corresponding to the cliques in the Soviet Party, but each slightly influencing the other. We had this, of course, at the time of the tussle between Malenkov and Khrushchev; we know from some of the published papers of Nagy that they were involved in the argument between Nagy and Rákosi in 1953.

LABEDZ: But there will also be some factions, like the Partisan faction in Poland, which will have no opposite numbers in the Soviet Party.

SETON-WATSON: Yes, there is nothing static about these factions; they are like molecules that come together and then disintegrate again. Cliques will come and cliques will go; we shall know about some of them, and not about others; and there will be a certain connection between the formation of these cliques in a given satellite and that of cliques in Moscow. Not in the sense that Faction A in Moscow promptly calls into being a new Faction A in Prague, or vice versa, but rather that the various like-minded particles start moving around each other's orbits——

LABEDZ: Looking for support——

SETON-WATSON: Yes.

LABEDZ: But of course if a 'satellite' régime chooses to use this time of stress to play what may be called a 'Rumanian gambit', to play, that is, the issue of national communism as a popular move in its own country with a view to winning greater autonomy *vis-à-vis* Moscow—then in that case it cannot afford to be identified with any Muscovite faction at all.

SETON-WATSON: I think we must also reckon with the possibility of the priorities being switched—of an East European régime, that is, not using traditional nationalist issues to achieve autonomy from Moscow, but using the growing opportunity of such autonomy to espouse the old nationalist war-cries for their own sake.

LABEDZ: Or at least for the sake of their own survival as a régime?

SETON-WATSON: Yes, one need not assume any great idealism; the effect would be the same.

LASKY: Do you think this is happening anywhere yet?

SETON-WATSON: I think there are symptoms which could facilitate this kind of trend. Take Rumania and the Transylvanian problem. The Rumanian régime has used its new 'freedom of manœuvre' not to be more liberal internally but rather to be more chauvinistic in its treatment of the Hungarian minority, which there is reason to believe is causing a great deal of resentment in Hungary itself. Now it might be that if the new Soviet leaders were infuriated beyond endurance by this Rumanian behaviour, they would give support to Hungarian nationalism; or that the Hungarian Party, as a price for supporting this or that candidate in Moscow, or for supporting any candidate's policy against China, might demand more Russian support for the Hungarian side over Transylvania.

The same sort of thing would crop up over Bulgaria and the Macedonian question. We saw how the Chinese resented Moscow's failure to help them to recover, or annex, Formosa. Well, the Bulgarians have two Formosas: one in Greece and one in Yugoslavia.

Where else in Europe, I wonder, could old nationalist claims be revived? The Poles' claims agains Germany have been satisfied, though Gomulka tries to exploit this argument still, with his interminable play-backs of the gramophone record about 'German revanchism'. They do of course have claims at the opposite point of the compass, but perhaps we have not really got to the stage yet where a communist government would start muttering aloud about Lwow or Vilno ...

LABEDZ: No, and I doubt whether we have even got to the point where the Russians would think it worth while stirring up trouble over Transylvania. This would really be a desperate measure; for if they seriously wanted to bring Transylvania on to the agenda, they would implicitly be setting a question-mark against their own acquisition of Bessarabia, and the Rumanians would have to retaliate by underlining this question-mark. They have already hinted at it by republishing an old article by Marx on the 'Eastern Question,' condemning Russia for the seizure of Bessarabia.

But since we have mentioned this matter of Soviet imperialism, I would suggest that the Russians are faced with something like the following choice of policies. They are still, despite the recent downgrading of ideology, involved in the international communist movement to an extent that distinguishes them from imperialists of the old-fashioned sort; they cannot entirely base their policies on a slogan of 'What I have, I hold'. They are still trying to do much more than this, and this has now led them into a fight on two fronts—the western side and the Chinese front—at a time when they have lost prestige and authority through the dismissal of Khrushchev. There is, therefore, perhaps more temptation than there has been for a long time for the Russians to give way to provocation, cut their losses and concentrate on consolidating their hold in Eastern Europe.

LASKY: I think this is a possibility that has to be taken very seriously. For there is a further point. Militarily, economically, geographically, the Soviets are paramount in Eastern Europe; the Chinese factor as an element in the satellite communists' manœuvring power is as strong as the Soviets allow it to be, and no more. That is to say, to the extent that the Soviets pay attention to the international movement and its leaders' opinions, to that extent the Rumanians and any other pro-Chinese groups in Eastern Europe have a measure of elbow-room. But why should the Soviets continue to pay attention? Why should they risk losing an empire in the hand for an empire in the bush, so to speak—the bush of Africa and the jungle of Asia? How long can the new Soviet leaders resist the conclusion that the old type of International is defunct; that it has become what Lenin derisively called a 'letterbox International'?

SETON-WATSON: The temptation may be clear, but so are the dangers—the dangers for the Soviets in trying to set up a tsarist-style empire in Eastern Europe and leaving the field of international debate to the Chinese, if that is what you are suggesting. Either way, they are not going to escape from the basic contradiction, as Marxists would say, between what the Russians preach and what they practise; between their anti-colonialist demagogy from Congo to Cuba, and their colonial practice from East Berlin to Mongolia. It is a grim and astonishing, not to say shaming, irony that the West has never yet made any effective protest, at the United Nations, against the fact that the Soviet Union exploits tens of millions of Central Asiatic Turks—Uzbeks, Kazakhs, etc.—in a colonial régime, not to mention Eastern Europe. And I have no doubt that it is going to fall to the Chinese of all people to pillory the Russians with no inhibitions at all—the Chinese who have a colonial empire of their own, including Turks and all.

LABEDZ: But I think we have failed to mention the real reason why the Russians continue to hold 'universalist' ambitions instead of sitting back as old-fashioned imperialists. It is not just inertia or a fondness for the old tunes and phrases, but the type of legitimacy on which the rule of the communist party rests. In this case, you cannot change your foreign policy simply because you have decided you are trying to bite off more than you can chew. It would be a sensible decision in itself, but if, as a side-effect, you would also have to abandon your domestic power structure, then the problem is more difficult. You have to keep a balance between domestic and foreign considerations, to change internally just as you are changing externally. What sort of internal changes should we expect in a Russia that is changing its foreign policy under the impact of what we have been discussing—possible disillusion with the whole over-inflated myth of the 'letterbox International'?

SETON-WATSON: We should expect the sort of changes we already see: a continued discrediting of the world-revolutionary argument for the party's 'vanguard' role. But though this will injure the party's prestige, it need not be a fatal blow. There are plenty of other, domestic justifications for the 'guiding role' of the CPSU—the tremendous successes of the economy and all that; they may be nonsense, but they are used.

LABEDZ: So the Russians may follow the Rumanians in taking the wind out of the nationalists' sails and play Great Russian chauvinism as against China, or as a claim for hegemony in Eastern Europe——

SETON-WATSON: But they did that already, in the last war.

LABEDZ: Yes, they did it then, but they were also clinging to the central doctrine of the struggle between socialism and capitalism——

LASKY: Which they need not abandon, any more than the church needs to denounce doctrines which are merely obsolescent. Moscow does not need to be consistent. For twenty years Stalin's main theme was building socialism 'in one country'; yet at the same time the Russians controlled a world-wide Comintern and ousted local leaders in France or America by *fiat* from Moscow.

LABEDZ: Yes, but one thing has changed. The Russians had no rival for the guidance of the International at that time. Now they have— the Chinese.

SETON-WATSON: In any case, the central doctrine you have mentioned, that of the struggle between socialism and capitalism, is not so very obsolescent—or need not appear to be. Every day revolutionary or quasi-revolutionary situations are going to crop up, in Africa, in South America and so on, which may or may not be communist-organized but which the Russians will leap in to furnish with Leninist interpretations. Perhaps in one respect we shall see a general change in Soviet policy here. Anti-white racialism is very evident in the Congo and elsewhere today. Racialism of the anti-Semitic sort: 'He's a white man. Exterminate him!' Now, are the Russians going to encourage this sort of thing? It is obviously not in their interest to do so, and with the Chinese standing by to support the fanatical elements, I think the dilemma must be worrying them.

LASKY: I am firmly convinced that the doctrinal element in Soviet policy is merely a form, an outer shell; not for thirty years and more has it been a matter of serious concern in Moscow whether a revolution will succeed in some far-off country. Or a counter-revolution, I should add, seeing that during the Spanish War the Soviets decided it was in their interest to suppress the socialist revolution by means of a bourgeois popular-front counter-revolution——

SETON-WATSON: But only to win the war, I think.

LASKY: Yes, to serve their interests——

SETON-WATSON: ——not their long-term interests——

LASKY: Perhaps; but that is hindsight. My point is that in every case it is the repercussions of a policy on the interests of the Soviet empire which have determined the decisions. And if the Chinese get a foothold in South Vietnam or in Africa, the Russians will object not out of doctrinal indignation that the revolution should be taking a path they consider revisionist or less Marxist or whatever, but simply because such victories will give the Chinese added strength: diplomatic, ideological, but especially physical strength and enhanced ability to press upon the Soviet Union as one territorial empire, one land mass, presses on another.

LABEDZ: I think everyone would agree with you that doctrine is not the cause of political tension, but the form. All the same, it is important. The strength of the Soviet Union was always greater than the strength of a single state, or of an empire, for it had the added support of the international communist movement. The Soviet leaders have had to justify their ability to wield this disproportionate influence, and ideology was the means to justify it. But once adopted, this ideology could not be abandoned without loss of the extra power that made Soviet foreign policy possible.

SETON-WATSON: But how valuable an asset is this ideology? There is a good deal of evidence, isn't there, that Stalin felt complete contempt for it and for the international revolutionaries who professed it.

LABEDZ: Yes—but he despised them not because of the particular ideology they held to, but because he knew they would dance as he sang. Well, what worked for Stalin would not work for Khrushchev, still less for the present leaders. And who will the leaders be in a year's time?

SETON-WATSON: We cannot tell how soon the succession crisis will be solved, nor—we may be sure—can the ringleaders themselves tell. Remember how deceptive appearances were after Stalin's death. The first phase ended soon with Malenkov apparently on top; then Beria fell; then finally Malenkov himself went...four years it took for the dust to settle.

LABEDZ: What I am really after is the effect upon the whole movement of a long, or a short, succession crisis in Moscow. These struggles make a sorry mess of the party's mystique, its legitimation. After all, the present tally is that out of forty-seven years of the Soviet Communist Party's history, forty were years of incorrect leadership, three decades of a big 'personality cult', and a decade of a small 'personality cult'.

SETON-WATSON: Wait a moment, Stalin was all right up to the end of collectivisation—I mean starving five million Soviet peasants was quite in order——

LABEDZ: Oh, but not even collectivisation is such a clear-cut issue now. Everything in the Soviet past is back in the historians' melting point. As the Radio Erevan joke has it, to predict the future is easy, but it is terribly hard to predict the Soviet past!

LASKY: The only easy prediction about the future that occurs to me is this: that amid all the fluidity and manœuvring that the succession struggle will doubtless bring, the various factions will all tend to be pushed to extremes, to adopt unreasonable versions of reasonable positions. You will get one faction saying, and even believing, that needless militancy and the creation of false tensions were responsible for the international difficulties in which the Soviet Union now finds itself; while on the other hand there will be advocates of toughness and no *détente*. We saw that in the episodes involving Beria, with Beria struggling to maintain his lead and even proposing to embrace adventurist disengagement policies in Eastern Europe—policies far more advanced, if reports are to be believed, than any other respons-ible Soviet politician had ever contemplated.

But is there, I wonder, a chance that what emerges from the other end of the crisis will be, not this extreme or that, but a 'centrist' policy that will look coldly at the world, allow of many roads to communism, and eschew dogmatism as not only silly but harmful to the state? I doubt it; but I don't see what other policy could hope to cope with the Sino-Soviet entanglement.

LABEDZ: Otherwise, you think the dialectics of the succession will lead to a new Time of Troubles, as in seventeenth century Tsarist Russia?

SETON-WATSON: Not quite as bad as that, I hope, for all our sakes.

LASKY: But there are historic parallels. The Roman empire split into East and West; but the process did not stop there. No doubt the Chinese will intrigue to hasten up the fissiparous effects; and no doubt the Russians will try to manœuvre in the same way in the 'Byzantine' half, I mean in the Chinese——

SETON-WATSON: But the balance is so much against them; China has its minorities but on the whole it is an ethnic unity. Whereas the Soviet Union proper is only about 50 per cent Russian, and then come all the non-Russian satellites. Yes, no doubt each side will try to exploit nationalism within the other camp—but it is really rather hard to imagine a *need* for the encouragement of Eastern European nationalism by conspicuously un-European-looking agents from Peking!

LABEDZ: What then, Seton-Watson, do you expect to happen in Eastern Europe in the post-Khrushchevian situation? Will it be a time of movement and opportunities seized, or of stagnation and opportunities lost?

SETON-WATSON: Assuming a period of weak and confusing leadership in Moscow, I should really think things might continue for a while roughly as they are. Perhaps in Czechoslovakia an already unpopular Novotny, needing and no longer getting protection from Moscow, might find himself ousted. But I can't imagine the even more unpopular Ulbricht being shifted from East Germany. Rumania I imagine will do better than ever; Hungary will continue to have the most liberal régime in the area, I suspect.

LABEDZ: What do you foresee, Lasky?

LASKY: I do feel that the next few years will be a kind of crossroads for Eastern Europe. We seem to be witnessing a race between two different and possibly conflicting trends. There is the evolution of the various East European régimes towards autonomy. And on the other hand there is the growing need for the Russians to make a choice between their universalist interests and their narrower imperial interests. By the time the Russians choose, and want perhaps to opt for consolidating their East European domains, they may find that it is too late to try.

LABEDZ: You mean the forces of nationalism will have broken up the East European part of the Soviet empire into its original parts?

SETON-WATSON: 'Original'? You mean into the various small states as they were in that brief period of independence between the collapse of the Hapsburg, Romanov and Ottoman empires, and the creation of the Soviet communist one?

LASKY: Plus or minus various territorial revisions at the expense of the Soviet Union, or of each other . . .? This sounds like the 'Balkanisation' that left-wing politicians speak of with horror in Africa.

SETON-WATSON: Yes, nationalism is a two-faced thing; sometimes it wears the face of Garibaldi, sometimes the face of the Commandant of Auschwitz; and it is none the better for being proclaimed by a small group—small groups, alas, can always find smaller ones to discriminate against. Strong feelings of national identity served the peoples of central and Eastern Europe well during their early struggles for independence, and have done so again under the Soviet empire. But excessive emphasis on separate national sovereignties proved quite disastrous between the wars.

LABEDZ: And could do so again, you are implying? Are you hinting at the need for some Danubian or East European Federation?

SETON-WATSON: It would be an impertinence for us in the West to start prescribing particular solutions. I am only anxious that people in the Danubian countries and their near neighbours should have the widest opportunities to learn, for example, of the similar problems that Western Europe has been wrestling with in the past decade; the problems of combining large and small countries together into bigger units without oppression or violation of feelings, simply for practical common ends. It would be difficult to think of any combination of circumstances that would relieve the future leaders of a free Eastern Europe of the responsibility to pool their resources and harmonize their national lives in some generous scheme of cooperation.

LABEDZ: I agree. Just as patriotism can be the last refuge of the scoundrel, nationalism can be the last refuge of the fool. Hitler and Mussolini exploited local nationalism in the Balkans; the communists have done the same whenever it suited them. Now nationalism is proving a weapon against them. But it is a crude weapon that too easily takes the form of an irrational prejudice. Once they have shaken off the dead dogmas and institutions of an imposed communism, the men and women of Eastern Europe should have more intelligent work to do than revive old frontier disputes. A new sanity—that is what is needed. And a breath of fresh air for everyone—Russians and Chinese included. Thank you, gentlemen.

Postscript

Leopold Labedz

After Khrushchev's fall a pathetic attempt was made by the new Soviet leaders to avoid the harsh historical choices facing them. They wanted to achieve a *détente* with China without giving up the fundamental Soviet interests in the dispute, but the Chinese were not interested in an agreement which would leave the Soviet position basically unaffected. They wanted a cake; the Russians wanted to have it and to eat it too.

The Chinese were, of course, eager to exploit Khrushchev's dismissal. At first, they played it cautiously in order to derive maximum advantage from the Soviet 'compromise' moves and conciliatory gestures. Unlike the Albanians, who never ceased to attack Khrushchev's successors with the same vehemence with which they had castigated the deposed leader, the Chinese limited themselves to reprinting 'anti-revisionist' polemics by pro-Chinese communists, generally avoiding direct abuse of the new Soviet leaders. Only with the approach of the March 1 conference did the rumblings in the Chinese press grow louder. To create the impression that the Russians were continuing the anti-Chinese polemics the Chinese press began once again to publish long lists of Soviet 'revisionist' articles, and made a great hue and cry about the publication of a book on the international communist movement by Boris Ponomarev, which had in fact been written and sent to press before Khrushchev's dismissal. In much the same way as they had done when Khrushchev called for an end to the open dispute in 1962, the Chinese used the alleged continuation of anti-Chinese polemics by the Russians as a pretext for stepping up their own anti-Soviet campaign.

Moreover, after Khrushchev's downfall the Chinese went ahead with the publication of the third, fourth and fifth volumes of *Statements by Khrushchev* as the best examples of the pitfalls of 'revisionism'. The last volume, covering 1956, did not include Khrushchev's 'secret speech', an interesting exception which can be formally justified by the fact that it has not been published in the Soviet Union. In the preface to this volume (published in April, 1965) the 20th CPSU Congress was described as one that would 'stink for all time' and Khrushchev and his successors were harshly condemned for adhering to the line laid down at that congress.

However, the first open censure of the new Soviet leaders came in a most violent form, on 23 March 1965, with the publication of 'A Comment on the March Moscow Meeting' in *Renmin Ribao* and *Hongqi*. The Chinese reply to the declaration of the Moscow meeting 'in favour of discounting the open polemics' could not be more vehement and uncompromising:

'It is the leaders of the CPSU themselves who started the public polemics in complete violation of the principles guiding relations among fraternal parties. . . . So far we have published only a small number of articles in reply to the attacks and slanders levelled at us by the leaders of the CPSU and their followers and we are a long way from having completed our replies, while in many cases we have not yet made any reply at all. Unless they openly announce the withdrawal of these anti-Chinese resolutions, statements and articles, and publicly admit their mistakes, it will be absolutely impossible to silence us. . . . Since modern revisionists have maligned us so much and refused to acknowledge their mistakes, it goes without saying that we have the right to refute them publicly. In these circumstances, it will not do to call for an end to the public polemics, it will not do to stop for a single day, for a month, a year, a hundred years, a thousand years, or ten thousand years. If nine thousand years are not enough to complete the refutation, then we shall take ten thousand.'

The new Soviet leadership was denounced in no uncertain terms:

'By playing tricks, the new leaders of the CPSU seemingly made some changes and a number of Khrushchev's original aims, which were based on wishful thinking, have not been fulfilled. But, in essence, the new leaders of the CPSU have taken over Khrushchev's revisionism and splittism lock, stock, and barrel, and they carried out his behest for a divisive meeting very faithfully. . . . If the new leaders of the CPSU really wanted unity and not a continuation of Khrushchev's old practice of plotting sham unity and a genuine split, why did they not . . . abandon this illegal schismatic meeting, change their direction, and make a fresh start? . . . In replacing Khrushchev they simply changed the signboard and employed more cunning methods and subterfuges in order to push through and develop Khrushchevism, and to carry out the general line of revisionism, great-power chauvinism, and splittism which Khrushchev had put forward at the 20th Congress of the CPSU, systematized at its 22nd Congress, and embodied in the programme of the CPSU.'

Khrushchev's successors were specifically condemned for 'capitulation to US imperialism' and the continuation of his hostile policy 'against China, Albania, the Japanese Communist Party, the Indonesian Communist Party, the New Zealand Communist Party, and all the fraternal countries and parties which uphold Marxism-Leninism'. They were also accused of interference in internal affairs of other parties and castigated for continuing to give 'strenuous support to the clique headed by Dange, that renegade from the Indian working class and running-dog of the Indian big bourgeoisie'. To sum up the damnation:

> 'What the new leaders of the CPSU have been doing can be described as "three shams and three realities": sham anti-imperialism but real capitulation, sham revolution but real betrayal, sham unity but a real split.'

The only way left for the Soviet leaders—which is 'at once difficult and not difficult'—is what in effect amounts to an unconditional surrender. They should make a public admission of errors on five counts:

1. That orders for the 'divisive' and 'schismatic' Moscow meeting were wrong and illegal.
2. That Khrushchev's 'revisionism, great-power chauvinism, and splittism' were wrong.
3. That 'the revisionist line and programme adopted at the 20th and 22nd Congresses of the CPSU' were wrong.
4. That 'all the words and deeds of the Soviet Party leaders directed against China, Albania, the Japanese Communist Party and other Marxist-Leninist Parties' were wrong.
5. 'Publicly pledge to desist from the error of Khrushchev revisionism and return to the road of Marxism-Leninism, proletarian internationalism, and the revolutionary principles.'

However, as such a solemn declaration 'before the communists and the peoples of the world' was not likely to be forthcoming, on a more realistic plane Peking announced that a 'new stage' has been reached in the struggle between its own and the Soviet line in the internationalist communist movement:

> 'The grave action of the new leaders of the CPSU in calling the divisive meeting has given the Marxist–Leninist parties and the Marxists–Leninists of the world the right to take the initiative. There is all the more reason now why we should openly criticize and thoroughly expose the revisionist line of the new leaders of CPSU, give more vigorous support to the people's revolutionary movements and the revolutionary left in different countries, and promote the faster growth of the Marxist–Leninist forces and the unity of the international communist movement on the basis of Marxism–Leninism and revolution.'

This clarion-call for an intensified struggle in the international communist movement came after the Moscow meeting had contributed to a further loss of the Kremlin's control over the parties it once dominated. These parties saw the prospects of the world communist conference, advocated for so long by the Soviet Communist Party, being postponed to the Greek calends. In their own comment on the Moscow meeting (published in *Zeri i Popullit* on March 18, 1965) the Albanians noticed with glee that 'the Soviet revisionist leadership has not succeeded in "bringing to heel" the other revisionists' and that it failed to establish 'a common revisionist line'. They triumphantly referred to the absence of the Rumanian Communist Party and 'six other sister parties' from the meeting and said that as a result of 'the plight in which the revisionists find themselves' the final communiqué was 'pathetic'. They were of course no less vitriolic in their denunciation of Khrushchev's successors than the Chinese, and they also attributed to them all the sins committed by the deposed leader, i.e. being 'lackeys of imperialism', 'chauvinists', 'lackeys of the bourgeoisie', 'rabid anti-Marxists', 'worst splitters and plotters', 'traitors', and more besides.

It goes without saying that for the Albanians, who, unlike the Chinese, never relaxed their vehement attacks on the Soviet leadership, 'public polemics will only cease when modern revisionists are unmasked entirely and annihilated definitely'. There can be no vacillation:

'A wait-and-see attitude, hesitation, hopes, and illusions regarding a reconciliation and unity with the revisionists are at present more dangerous than ever, and they compromise seriously the vital interests of communists and of the revolutionary movement.'

Apart from some nuances, the Albanian denunciation of 'Khrushchevism without Khrushchev' coincided on all points with the Chinese one. It rejected

'the opportunist and revisionist line of the 20th, 21st and 22nd congresses, the line of alleged "peaceful coexistence", of "peaceful competition", of the "peaceful way" of "total and general disarmament", of "multilateral Soviet–American collaboration", of "anti-Stalinism", of the "state of the entire people" of the "party of the entire people", and so on and so forth.'

The Chinese document, published five days later, had this to say about the attempted *détente* in the Sino-Soviet relations by the new leaders:

'All their fine words only amount to selling horsemeat as a beefsteak; they are saying one thing and doing another. . . . Since the new leaders of the CPSU are now following Khrushchev's whole revisionist general line of "peaceful coexistence", "peaceful competition", "peaceful transition", "the state of the whole people", and "the party of the entire people", this only goes to prove that they are still bent on deepening the differences, wrecking unity, and doing fresh damage to the international communist movement.'

Thus, as should have been clear from the beginning, the 'new' Soviet policy towards China after Khrushchev has been a failure. The Chinese had never any intention of letting the Russians blunt the edge of their dilemmas, between party and state considerations, between the national and ideological interests, between Soviet internal development and the necessities of revolutionary movements in undeveloped countries. For Peking there was no question of half-measures; it demanded a complete Soviet capitulation on all points at issue because it wanted to present Moscow with a harsh alternative: either to back its own revolutionary line and contribute to the growth of the Chinese power or be branded as an accomplice of 'U S imperialism', a traitor to the revolutionary cause, lukewarm and half-hearted in its support for the 'national liberation movements'.

These terms were unacceptable to Moscow; it did not relish the prospect of becoming a Chinese satellite, nor did it want to abandon its claims to the leadership of the international communist movement by a return to traditional great power politics based simply on national interest. But its attempts at a compromise with Peking have not achieved even the minimum aim of improving state relations between the two countries. On the contrary, these deteriorated still further, while at the same time the Russians were paying the price of this unachievable compromise in having their once unchallengeable position in the international communist movement undermined more and more. Different categories of parties on the polycentric spectrum slipped ever further away from Moscow's influence. The pro-Chinese parties became more rigid in their uncompromising attitude; the neutralist parties more sure of themselves and more of a bad example for the vacillators. Rumania sneaked out of the Soviet grasp completely and boycotted the Moscow meeting. Cuba, much more dependent on Soviet help, was clearly reluctant to attend and confirmed, only a few days before the conference, that it would do so. It had already strayed away from a strictly neutral position when it signed the pro-Soviet communiqué of the 1964 Havana conference of Latin American communist parties, which it was eager to prevent from ending in a fiasco. But after the Moscow meeting, to which he sent his brother Raul, Fidel Castro gave vent to his suppressed feelings in a speech on March 13, 1965, when he proclaimed again his ideological independence *vis-à-vis* the two communist giants. He said in effect, 'A plague on both your houses', pointedly insisting that 'Cuba needs no lessons in revolutionary spirit from anybody' and warning those who may 'dare to doubt' it that he will 'drive from our country, from the ranks of our people, these disputes, these Byzantine feuds'.*

Among the vacillating parties, the British delegate came only after the Moscow meeting had already begun, and the Polish delegate had apparently been too close to the Italian line for Soviet comfort. The final communiqué of the Moscow meeting bears unmistakable traces of the Italian Communist Party's dislike of a central direction in the communist movement. As the Albanians put it, it represents in fact 'a triumph of the revisionist Togliatti's theses and tactics clearly outlined in the "testament" of Palmiro Togliatti who came out against the monocentrist line of the Soviet leadership ... and ... for avoiding, as far as possible, a full split and an open confrontation with the Marxists-Leninists, of which they are in mortal fear'.

On their part, the Chinese communists continued their polemics. Two years after their original doctrinal challenge, *Renmin Ribao* and *Hongqi* devoted to it an anniversary article, stressing again that the struggle against 'modern revisionism' must be intensified. It said that 'Marxists-Leninists' must base themselves on the lessons of the struggle of Lenin against the Second International, of Stalin's fight with Trotsky and Bukharin, and of the experience accumulated in combating Khrushchev. His successors also have to be fought to the end, being like him,

'the representatives of the bourgeois privileged stratum in the Soviet Union who cannot but act in the interest of this stratum and to pursue the revisionist line. On this fundamental question they cannot be different from Khrushchev. That is why for the last eight months they have had permanent difficulties and have been constantly contradicting themselves.'

A few days later *Pravda* (June 20, 1965) indicated that Soviet patience was nearly exhausted. It said that since October 1964 the Soviet Communist Party had refrained from open polemics, but 'unfortunately this attitude has not been correctly appreciated by the Chinese Communist Party leadership'. It argued that China's intransigence was a betrayal of the interests of international communism.

Thus eight months after Khrushchev's downfall the two sides found themselves again almost at square one. The struggle continues and it is more and more difficult for the Russians to maintain silence in the face of the continuing shrill condemnations by the Chinese. But their resumption of open polemics can only mean that the Sino-Soviet conflict will flare up with renewed vigour.

* After the fall of Ben Balla, the Belgian pro-Chinese weekly, *La Voix du Peuple* (July) 2, 1965) criticized Castro for his hostile attitude towards the règime of Colonel Boumedienne.

Contributors

W. A. C. ADIE is a Research Fellow of St. Antony's College, Oxford, and a student of Chinese and African affairs.

GORDON BARRASS, formerly on the editorial staff of *The Economist*, is assistant editor of *The China Quarterly*. He has written extensively on Far Eastern affairs.

R. V. BURKS, formerly Professor of History at Wayne State University, is Policy Director of Radio Free Europe. His publications include *The Dynamics of Communism in Eastern Europe*.

ROBERT CONQUEST has written *Common Sense about Russia, The Pasternak Affair, Power and Policy in the USSR, The Soviet Deportation of Nationalities, Marxism Today*, etc.

BRIAN CROZIER, formerly of *The Economist*, is the author of *The Rebels, The Morning After*, and *Neo-Colonialism*.

JANE DEGRAS is on the staff of the Royal Institute of International Affairs, Chatham House, London, and editor of *Soviet Documents on Foreign Policy, 1917–1941* (3 vols.); *The Communist International 1919–43: Documents*.

KEVIN DEVLIN, formerly on the editorial staff of *The Guardian*, is a senior political analyst with Radio Free Europe. He has written and published extensively on problems of communism.

DAVID FLOYD is the principal correspondent for communist affairs of *The Daily Telegraph* and author of i.a. *Hostile Partners: a short history of Sino-Soviet relations*.

WILLIAM E. GRIFFITH is Research Associate at the Massachusetts Institute of Technology and author of *Albania and the Sino-Soviet Rift, The Sino-Soviet Rift*, etc.

RICHARD ROCKINGHAM GILL, formerly on the staff of the British Embassy in Moscow (1948–50), subsequently worked for the Foreign Office for a further four years in London and Vienna; he is senior Soviet analyst with Radio Free Europe.

PATRICK J. HONEY is Reader in Vietnamese at the London School of Oriental and African Studies. He has been visiting Vietnam over the last 20 years. He writes and broadcasts frequently on Vietnamese affairs and is the author of *Communism in North Vietnam*.

G. F. HUDSON is Head of the Far Eastern Institute at St. Antony's College, Oxford. His publications include: *Europe and China; World after Hitler; Sino-Soviet Dispute* (with others) and *Far Eastern Affairs* I and II (editor).

LEOPOLD LABEDZ is associate editor of *Survey*, and editor of the Library of International Studies. Publications: *Revisionism* (editor); *Literature and Revolution in Soviet Russia, 1917–62* (editor with Max Hayward); *Polycentrism* (editor with Walter Laqueur); *The Future of Communist Society* (editor with Walter Laqueur); *Khrushchev and the Arts* (editor with Priscilla Johnson).

MELVIN J. LASKY is editor (with Stephen Spender) of *Encounter*, and author of *Africa for Beginners* and *A White Book, the Hungarian Revolution* (editor).

RICHARD LOWENTHAL is Professor of International Relations at the Otto-Suhr Institute of Berlin University and author of *World Communism: The Disintegration of a Secular Faith*.

RODERICK MACFARQUHAR is editor of *China Quarterly* and author of *The Hundred Flowers* and *The Sino-Soviet Dispute* (with G. F. Hudson and Richard Lowenthal).

DAVID L. MORISON is editor of *Mizan News Letter*, a monthly review of Soviet writings on the Middle East and Africa. He is author of *The USSR and Africa*.

LEONARD SCHAPIRO is Professor of Political Science with special reference to Russian Studies at the London School of Economics and Political Science and author of *The Communist Party of the Soviet Union*.

HUGH SETON-WATSON is Professor of Russian History at the University of London and author of *Eastern Europe between the Wars*, *The Decline of Imperial Russia*, *The Pattern of Communist Revolution*, *Neither War nor Peace*, and *The New Imperialism*.

ALFRED SHERMAN, at one time *Observer* special correspondent in Belgrade, is the author of several studies on the Middle East, Eastern Europe, Latin America and China.

G. R. URBAN, Head of University Broadcasting, Radio Free Europe, is the author of *The Nineteen Days: A Broadcaster's Account of the Hungarian Revolution*, *Kinesis and Stasis: A Study in the Attitude of Stefan George and his Circle to the Musical Arts*, and *Talking to Eastern Europe: A Collection of the Best Reading from the Broadcasts and Background Papers of Radio Free Europe* (editor).

DERYCK VINEY, a former member of the research staff of Radio Free Europe (1951–63), studied Czech at Cambridge and Prague where he obtained his Ph.D. for a thesis on Josef Capek's writings. His publications include studies of the impact of communism on the Czech cultural scene.

HARRY WILLETTS is a Research Fellow of St. Antony's College, Oxford, and a writer on Soviet and communist affairs.

DONALD S. ZAGORIA is a member of the Social Science Department of the RAND Corporation where he specializes in Sino-Soviet relations, and Assistant Professor of Government at Columbia University, New York. He has contributed articles to *Problems of Communism*, *The New Leader*, *The Asian Survey*, and *Survey*. Publications: *The Sino-Soviet Conflict* (1956–61) and *Communist China and the Soviet Bloc* (editor).

THE SINO-SOVIET CONFLICT